CAMBRIDGE LIBRARY COLLECTION

Books of enduring scholarly value

English Men of Letters

In the 1870s, Macmillan publishers began to issue a series of books called 'English Men of Letters' – biographies of English writers by other English writers. The general editor of the series was the journalist, critic, politician, and supporter (and later biographer) of Gladstone, John Morley (1838–1923). The aim was to provide a short introduction to each subject and his works, but also that the life should illuminate the works, and vice versa. The subjects range chronologically from Chaucer to Thackeray and Dickens, and an important feature of the series is that many of the authors (Henry James on Hawthorne, Ward on Dickens) were discussing writers of the previous generation, and some (Trollope on Thackeray) had even known their subjects personally. The series exemplifies the British approach to literary biography and criticism at the end of the nineteenth century, and also reveals which authors were at that time regarded as canonical.

Swift

Sir Leslie Stephen (1832–1904) came from a distinguished family of politicians, jurists and writers, and was the father of Vanessa Bell and Virginia Woolf. His literary career began with writing about his great passion, the Alps, and he became a noted author and critic, and the first editor of the *Dictionary of National Biography*. He was a friend of John Morley (1838–1923), the general editor of English Men of Letters, who commissioned him to write three biographies for the first series, on Swift, Pope and Johnson. Stephen is very interested in the family connections and history of Jonathan Swift (1667–1745), the great satirist and moralist, and he blends direct sources with general conclusions in an informal style which makes the work (first published in 1882) of continuing interest today. Stephen's *Sketches from Cambridge*, published anonymously in 1865, is also reissued in the Cambridge Library Collection.

T0370570

Cambridge University Press has long been a pioneer in the reissuing of out-of-print titles from its own backlist, producing digital reprints of books that are still sought after by scholars and students but could not be reprinted economically using traditional technology. The Cambridge Library Collection extends this activity to a wider range of books which are still of importance to researchers and professionals, either for the source material they contain, or as landmarks in the history of their academic discipline.

Drawing from the world-renowned collections in the Cambridge University Library, and guided by the advice of experts in each subject area, Cambridge University Press is using state-of-the-art scanning machines in its own Printing House to capture the content of each book selected for inclusion. The files are processed to give a consistently clear, crisp image, and the books finished to the high quality standard for which the Press is recognised around the world. The latest print-on-demand technology ensures that the books will remain available indefinitely, and that orders for single or multiple copies can quickly be supplied.

The Cambridge Library Collection will bring back to life books of enduring scholarly value (including out-of-copyright works originally issued by other publishers) across a wide range of disciplines in the humanities and social sciences and in science and technology.

Swift

L ESLIE S TEPHEN

CAMBRIDGE UNIVERSITY PRESS

CAMBRIDGE UNIVERSITY PRESS

Cambridge, New York, Melbourne, Madrid, Cape Town,
Singapore, São Paolo, Delhi, Tokyo, Mexico City

Published in the United States of America by Cambridge University Press, New York

www.cambridge.org
Information on this title: www.cambridge.org/9781108034494

© in this compilation Cambridge University Press 2011

This edition first published 1882
This digitally printed version 2011

ISBN 978-1-108-03449-4 Paperback

𝔈nglish 𝔐en of 𝔏etters

EDITED BY JOHN MORLEY

SWIFT

SWIFT

BY

LESLIE STEPHEN

London:

MACMILLAN AND CO.

1882

PREFACE.

THE chief materials for a life of Swift are to be found in his writings and correspondence. The best edition is the second of the two edited by Scott (1814 and 1824).

In 1751 Lord Orrery published *Remarks upon the Life and Writings of Dr. Jonathan Swift.* Orrery, born 1707, had known Swift from about 1732. His remarks give the views of a person of quality of more ambition than capacity, and more anxious to exhibit his own taste than to give full or accurate information.

In 1754, Dr. Delany published *Observations upon Lord Orrery's Remarks*, intended to vindicate Swift against some of Orrery's severe judgments. Delany, born about 1685, became intimate with Swift soon after the dean's final settlement in Ireland. He was then one of the authorities of Trinity College, Dublin. He is the best contemporary authority, so far as he goes.

In 1756 Deane Swift, grandson of Swift's uncle Godwin, and son-in-law to Swift's cousin and faithful guardian, Mrs. Whiteway, published an *Essay upon the Life, Writings, and Character of Dr. Jonathan Swift*, in which he attacks both his predecessors. Deane Swift, born about 1708, had seen little or nothing of his cousin till the year 1738, when the dean's faculties were decaying. His book is foolish and discursive. Deane Swift's son, Theophilus, communicated a good deal of doubtful matter to Scott, on the authority of family tradition.

In 1765 Hawkesworth, who had no personal knowledge, prefixed a life of Swift to an edition of the works which adds nothing to our information. In 1781 Johnson, when publishing a very perfunctory life of Swift as one of the poets, excused its shortcomings on the ground of having already communicated his thoughts to Hawkesworth. The life is not only meagre but injured by one of Johnson's strong prejudices.

In 1785 Thomas Sheridan produced a pompous and dull life of Swift. He was the son of Swift's most intimate companion during the whole period subsequent to the final settlement in Ireland. The elder Sheridan, however, died in 1738; and the younger, born in 1721, was still a boy when Swift was becoming imbecile.

Contemporary writers, except Delany, have thus little authority; and a number of more or less palpably fictitious anecdotes accumulated round their hero. Scott's life, originally published in 1814, is defective in point of accuracy. Scott did not investigate the evidence minutely, and liked a good story too well to be very particular about its authenticity. The book, however, shows his strong sense and genial appreciation of character; and remains, till this day, by far the best account of Swift's career.

A life which supplies Scott's defects in great measure was given by William Monck Mason, in 1819, in his *History and Antiquities of the Church of St. Patrick.* Monck Mason was an indiscriminate admirer, and has a provoking method of expanding undigested information into monstrous notes, after the precedent of Bayle. But he examined facts with the utmost care, and every biographer must respect his authority.

In 1875 Mr. Forster published the first instalment of a *Life of Swift.* This book, which contains the results of patient and thorough inquiry, was unfortunately interrupted by Mr. Forster's death, and ends at the beginning of 1711. A complete *Life* by Mr. Henry Craik is announced as about to appear.

Besides these books, I ought to mention an *Essay upon the Earlier Part of the Life of Swift,* by the Rev. John Barrett, B.D. and Vice-Provost of Trin. Coll. Dublin (London, 1808) ; and *The Closing Years of Dean Swift's Life,* by W. R. Wilde, M.R.I.A., F.R.C.S. (Dublin, 1849). This last is a very interesting study of the medical aspects of Swift's life. An essay by Dr. Bucknill, in *Brain* for Jan. 1882, is a remarkable contribution to the same subject.

CONTENTS.

SWIFT

SWIFT.

CHAPTER I.

EARLY YEARS.

JONATHAN SWIFT, the famous Dean of St. Patrick's, was the descendant of an old Yorkshire family. One branch had migrated southwards, and in the time of Charles I., Thomas Swift, Jonathan's grandfather, was Vicar of Goodrich, near Ross, in Herefordshire, a fact commemorated by the sweetest singer of Queen Ann's reign in the remarkable lines—

> Jonathan Swift
> Had the gift
> By fatherige, motherige,
> And by brotherige,
> To come from Gotheridge.

Thomas Swift married Elizabeth Dryden, niece of Sir Erasmus, the grandfather of the poet Dryden. By her he became the father of ten sons and four daughters. In the great rebellion he distinguished himself by a loyalty which was the cause of obvious complacency to his descendant. On one occasion he came to the governor of a town held for the king, and being asked what he could do for his Majesty, laid down his coat as an offering. The

B

governor remarked that his coat was worth little. "Then," said Swift, "take my waistcoat." The waistcoat was lined with three hundred broad pieces—a handsome offering from a poor and plundered clergyman. On another occasion he armed a ford, through which rebel cavalry were to pass, by certain pieces of iron with four spikes, so contrived that one spike must always be uppermost (*caltrops*, in short). Two hundred of the enemy were destroyed by this stratagem. The success of the rebels naturally led to the ruin of this cavalier clergyman; and the record of his calamities forms a conspicuous article in Walker's *Sufferings of the Clergy*. He died in 1658, before the advent of the better times in which he might have been rewarded for his loyal services. His numerous family had to struggle for a living. The eldest son, Godwin Swift, was a barrister of Gray's Inn at the time of the Restoration: he was married four times, and three times to women of fortune ; his first wife had been related to the Ormond family ; and this connexion induced him to seek his fortune in Ireland—a kingdom which at that time suffered, amongst other less endurable grievances, from a deficient supply of lawyers.[1] Godwin Swift was made Attorney-General in the palatinate of Tipperary by the Duke of Ormond. He prospered in his profession, in the subtle parts of which, says his nephew, he was "perhaps a little too dexterous ;" and he engaged in various speculations, having at one time what was then the very large income of 3000*l.* a year. Four brothers accompanied this successful Godwin, and shared to some extent in his prosperity. In January, 1666, one of these, Jonathan, married to Abigail Erick, of Leicester, was appointed to the stewardship of the King's Inns, Dublin, partly in consideration of the

---

[1] *Deane Swift*, p. 15.

loyalty and suffering of his family. Some fifteen months later, in April, 1667, he died, leaving his widow with an infant daughter, and seven months after her husband's death, November 30, 1667, she gave birth to Jonathan, the younger, at 7, Hoey's Court, Dublin.

The Dean "hath often been heard to say" (I quote his fragment of autobiography) "that he felt the consequences of that (his parents') marriage, not only through the whole course of his education, but during the greater part of his life." This quaint assumption that a man's parentage is a kind of removable accident to which may be attributed a limited part of his subsequent career, betrays a characteristic sentiment. Swift cherished a vague resentment against the fates which had mixed bitter ingredients in his lot. He felt the place as well as the circumstances of his birth to be a grievance. It gave a plausibility to the offensive imputation that he was of Irish blood. "I happened," he said, with a bitterness born of later sufferings, "by a perfect accident to be born here, and thus I am a Teague, or an Irishman, or what people please." Elsewhere he claims England as properly his own country; "although I happened to be dropped here, and was a year old before I left it (Ireland), and to my sorrow did not die before I came back to it." His infancy brought fresh grievances. He was, it seems, a precocious and delicate child, and his nurse became so much attached to him, that having to return to her native Whitehaven, she kidnapped the year-old infant out of pure affection. When his mother knew her loss, she was afraid to hazard a return voyage until the child was stronger; and he thus remained nearly three years at Whitehaven, where the nurse took such care of his education, that he could read any chapter in the Bible before he was three years old. His return must

have been speedily followed by his mother's departure for
her native Leicester.   Her sole dependence, it seems, was
an annuity of 20*l*. a year, which had been bought for her
by her husband upon their marriage.   Some of the Swift
family seem also to have helped her; but for reasons not
now discoverable, she found Leicester preferable to Dublin,
even at the price of parting from the little Jonathan.
Godwin took him off her hands and sent him to Kilkenny School at the age of six, and from that early
period the child had to grow up as virtually an orphan.
His mother through several years to come can have been
little more than a name to him.   Kilkenny School, called
the "Eton of Ireland," enjoyed a high reputation.   Two
of Swift's most famous contemporaries were educated
there.   Congreve, two years his junior, was one of his
schoolfellows, and a warm friendship remained when both
had become famous.   Fourteen years after Swift had left
the school it was entered by George Berkeley, destined to
win a fame of the purest and highest kind, and to come
into a strange relationship to Swift.   It would be vain to
ask what credit may be claimed by Kilkenny School for
thus " producing " (it is the word used on such occasions)
the greatest satirist, the most brilliant writer of comedies,
and the subtlest metaphysician in the English language.
Our knowledge of Swift's experiences at this period is
almost confined to a single anecdote.   "I remember," he
says incidentally in a letter to Lord Bolingbroke, " when I
was a little boy, I felt a great fish at the end of my line,
which I drew up almost on the ground ; but it dropped in,
and the disappointment vexes me to this very day, and I
believe it was the type of all my future disappointments." [2]

[2] Readers may remember a clever adaptation of this incident
in Lord Lytton's *My Novel.*

Swift, indeed, was still in the schoolboy stage, according to modern ideas, when he was entered at Trinity College, Dublin, on the same day, April 24, 1682, with a cousin, Thomas Swift. Swift clearly found Dublin uncongenial; though there is still a wide margin for uncertainty as to precise facts. His own account gives a short summary of his academic history :—

" By the ill-treatment of his nearest relations " (he says) " he was so discouraged and sunk in his spirits that he too much neglected his academic studies, for some parts of which he had no great relish by nature, and turned himself to reading history and poetry, so that when the time came for taking his degree of Bachelor of Arts, although he had lived with great regularity and due observance of the statutes, he was stopped of his degree for dulness and insufficiency; and at last hardly admitted in a manner little to his credit, which is called in that college *speciali gratia.*" In a report of one of the college examinations, discovered by Mr. Forster, he receives a *bene* for his Greek and Latin, a *male* for his " philosophy," and a *negligenter* for his theology. The " philosophy " was still based upon the old scholasticism, and proficiency was tested by skill in the arts of syllogistic argumentation. Sheridan, son of Swift's intimate friend, was a student at Dublin shortly before the Dean's loss of intellectual power; the old gentleman would naturally talk to the lad about his university recollections; and, according to his hearer, remembered with singular accuracy the questions upon which he had disputed, and repeated the arguments which had been used, " in syllogistic form." Swift at the same time declared, if the report be accurate, that he never had the patience to read the pages of Smiglecius, Burgersdicius, and the other old-fashioned logi-

cal treatises.   When told that they taught the art of reasoning, he declared that he could reason very well without it.
He acted upon this principle in his exercises, and left
the Proctor to reduce his argument to the proper form.
In this there is probably a substratum of truth. Swift
can hardly be credited, as Berkeley might have been, with
a precocious perception of the weakness of the accepted
system.   When young gentlemen are plucked for their
degree, it is not generally because they are in advance of their
age.   But the aversion to metaphysics was characteristic of
Swift through life.   Like many other people who have no
turn for such speculations, he felt for them a contempt
which may perhaps be not the less justified because
it does not arise from familiarity.   The bent of his mind
was already sufficiently marked to make him revolt against
the kind of mental food which was most in favour at
Dublin ; though he seems to have obtained a fair knowledge of the classics.

Swift cherished through life a resentment against
most of his relations. His uncle Godwin had under-
taken his education, and had sent him, as we see, to the
best places of education in Ireland. If the supplies
became scanty, it must be admitted that poor Godwin
had a sufficient excuse. Each of his four wives had
brought him a family—the last leaving him seven sons ;
his fortunes had been dissipated, chiefly, it seems, by
means of a speculation in iron-works ; and the poor man
himself seems to have been failing, for he " fell into a
lethargy " in 1688, surviving some five years, like his
famous nephew, in a state of imbecility.   Decay of mind
and fortune coinciding with the demands of a rising family
might certainly be some apology for the neglect of one
amongst many nephews. Swift did not consider it sufficient.   " Was it not your uncle Godwin," he was asked

"who educated you?"   "Yes," said Swift, after a pause ;
"he gave me the education of a dog."   "Then," answered
the intrepid inquirer, "you have not the gratitude of a
dog." And perhaps that is our natural impression. Yet
we do not know enough of the facts to judge with confidence. Swift, whatever his faults, was always a warm
and faithful friend ; and perhaps it is the most probable
conjecture that Godwin Swift bestowed his charity coldly
and in such a way as to hurt the pride of the recipient.
In any case, it appears that Swift showed his resentment
in a manner more natural than reasonable. The child is
tempted to revenge himself by knocking his head against
the rock which has broken his shins; and with equal wisdom
the youth who fancies that the world is not his friend, tries
to get satisfaction by defying its laws. Till the time of his
degree (February, 1686), Swift had been at least regular
in his conduct, and if the neglect of his relations had discouraged his industry, it had not provoked him to rebellion. During the three years which followed he became
more reckless. He was still a mere lad, just eighteen
at the time of his degree, when he fell into more or less
irregular courses.   In rather less than two years he
was under censure for seventy weeks. The offences consisted chiefly in neglect to attend chapel and in " town-
haunting " or absence from the nightly roll-call. Such
offences perhaps appear to be more flagrant than they
really are in the eyes of college authorities. Twice he got
into more serious scrapes. He was censured (March 16,
1687) along with his cousin, Thomas Swift, and several
others for "notorious neglect of duties and frequenting
'the town.'"   And on his twenty-first birthday (Nov. 30,
1688) he [3] was punished, along with several others, for

[3] Possibly this was his cousin Thomas, but the probabilities
are clearly in favour of Jonathan.

exciting domestic dissensions, despising the warnings of
the junior dean, and insulting that official by contemptuous words. The offenders were suspended from
their degrees, and inasmuch as Swift and another were
the worst offenders (*adhuc intolerabilius se gesserant*), they
were sentenced to ask pardon of the dean upon their
knees publicly in the hall. Twenty years later [4] Swift
revenged himself upon Owen Lloyd, the junior dean, by
accusing him of infamous servility. For the present Swift
was probably reckoned amongst the black sheep of the
academic flock. [5]

This censure came at the end of Swift's university career.
The three last years had doubtless been years of discouragement and recklessness. That they were also years
of vice in the usual sense of the word is not proved ; nor,
from all that we know of Swift's later history, does it
seem to be probable. There is no trace of anything like
licentious behaviour in his whole career. It is easier to
believe with Scott that Swift's conduct at this period
might be fairly described in the words of Johnson when
speaking of his own university experience : " Ah, sir, I
was mad and violent. It was bitterness that they mistook
for frolic. I was miserably poor, and I thought to fight
my way by my literature and my wit ; so I disregarded
all power and all authority." Swift learnt another and
a more profitable lesson in these years. It is indicated in

---

[4] In the *Short Character of Thomas, Earl of Wharton.*

[5] It will be seen that I accept Dr. Barrett's statements, *Earlier
Part of the Life of Swift*, pp. 13, 14. His arguments seem to me
sufficiently clear and conclusive, and they are accepted by Monck
Mason, though treated contemptuously by Mr. Forster, p. 34. On
the other hand, I agree with Mr. Forster that Swift's complicity in
the *Terræ Filius* oration is not proved, though it is not altogether
improbable.

an anecdote which rests upon tolerable authority.   One
day, as he was gazing in melancholy mood from his
window, his pockets at their lowest ebb, he saw a sailor
staring about in the college courts.   How happy should I
be, he thought, if that man was inquiring for me with a
present from my cousin Willoughby !   The dream came
true.   The sailor came to his rooms and produced a
leather bag, sent by his cousin from Lisbon, with more
money than poor Jonathan had ever possessed in his life.
The sailor refused to take a part of it for his trouble,
and Jonathan hastily crammed the money into his pocket,
lest the man should repent of his generosity.   From that
time forward, he added, he became a better economist.

The Willoughby Swift here mentioned was the eldest
son of Godwin, and now settled in the English factory
at Lisbon.   Swift speaks warmly of his " goodness and
generosity " in a letter written to another cousin in 1694.
Some help, too, was given by his uncle William, who was
settled at Dublin, and whom he calls the " best of his
relations."   In one way or another he was able to keep
his head above water ; and he was receiving an impression
which grew with his growth.   The misery of dependence
was burnt into his soul.   To secure independence became
his most cherished wish ; and the first condition of independence was a rigid practice of economy.   We shall see
hereafter how deeply this principle became rooted in his
mind ; here I need only notice that it is the lesson
which poverty teaches to none but men of strong character.

A catastrophe meanwhile was approaching, which involved the fortunes of Swift along with those of nations.
James II. had been on the throne for a year when Swift
took his degree.   At the time when Swift was ordered to
kneel to the junior dean, William was in England, and

James preparing to fly from Whitehall. The revolution
of 1688 meant a breaking up of the very foundations of
political and social order in Ireland. At the end of 1688
a stream of fugitives was pouring into England, whilst
the English in Ireland were gathering into strong places,
abandoning their property to the bands of insurgent
peasants.

Swift fled with his fellows. Any prospects which he
may have had in Ireland were ruined with the ruin of his
race. The loyalty of his grandfather to a king who protected the national church was no precedent for loyalty
to a king who was its deadliest enemy. Swift, a Churchman to the backbone, never shared the leaning of many
Anglicans to the exiled Stuarts; and his early experience
was a pretty strong dissuasive from Jacobitism. He took
refuge with his mother at Leicester. Of that mother we
hear less than we could wish; for all that we hear suggests a brisk, wholesome, motherly body. She lived
cheerfully and frugally on her pittance; rose early,
worked with her needle, read her book, and deemed
herself to be "rich and happy"—on twenty pounds a
year. A touch of her son's humour appears in the only
anecdote about her. She came, it seems, to visit her son
in Ireland shortly after he had taken possession of
Laracor, and amused herself by persuading the woman
with whom she lodged that Jonathan was not her son but
her lover. Her son, though separated from her through
the years in which filial affection is generally nourished,
loved her with the whole strength of his nature; he wrote
to her frequently, took pains to pay her visits "rarely less
than once a year;" and was deeply affected by her death
in 1710. "I have now lost," he wrote in his pocket-
book, "the last barrier between me and death. God

grant I may be as well prepared for it as I confidently
believe her to have been! If the way to Heaven be
through piety, truth, justice, and charity, she is there."

The good lady had, it would seem, some little
anxieties of the common kind about her son. She
thought him in danger of falling in love with a certain
Betty Jones, who, however, escaped the perils of being
wife to a man of genius, and married an innkeeper.
Some forty years later, Betty Jones, now Perkins, appealed
to Swift to help her in some family difficulties, and Swift
was ready to "sacrifice five pounds" for old acquaintance'
sake. Other vague reports of Swift's attentions to women
seem to have been flying about in Leicester. Swift, in
noticing them, tells his correspondent that he values "his
own entertainment beyond the obloquy of a parcel of
wretched fools," which he "solemnly pronounces" to be a
fit description of the inhabitants of Leicester. He had, he
admits, amused himself with flirtation; but he has learnt
enough, "without going half a mile beyond the University,"
to refrain from thoughts of matrimony. A "cold temper"
and the absence of any settled outlook are sufficient dis-
suasives. Another phrase in the same letter is characteristic. "A person of great honour in Ireland (who was
pleased to stoop so low as to look into my mind) used
to tell me that my mind was like a conjured spirit that
would do mischief if I did not give it employment."
He allowed himself these little liberties, he seems to
infer, by way of distraction for his restless nature. But
some more serious work was necessary, if he was to win
the independence so earnestly desired, and to cease to be
a burden upon his mother. Where was he to look for
help?

CHAPTER II.

How was this "conjured spirit" to find occupation?
The proverbial occupation of such beings is to cultivate
despair by weaving ropes of sand. Swift felt himself
strong ; but he had no task worthy of his strength : nor
did he yet know precisely where it lay : he even fancied
that it might be in the direction of Pindaric Odes.
Hitherto his energy had expended itself in the questionable
shape of revolt against constituted authority. But the
revolt, whatever its precise nature, had issued in the rooted
determination to achieve a genuine independence. The
political storm which had for the time crushed the whole
social order of Ireland into mere chaotic anarchy, had left
him an uprooted waif and stray—a loose fragment without
any points of attachment, except the little household in
Leicester. His mother might give him temporary shelter,
but no permanent home. If, as is probable, he already
looked forward to a clerical career, the Church to which
he belonged was, for the time, hopelessly ruined, and in
danger of being a persecuted sect.

In this crisis a refuge was offered to him. Sir William
Temple was connected, in more ways than one, with the
Swifts. He was the son of Sir John Temple, Master of
the Rolls in Ireland, who had been a friend of Godwin

Swift. Temple himself had lived in Ireland, in early days,
and had known the Swift family. His wife was in some
way related to Swift's mother; and he was now in a
position to help the young man. Temple is a remarkable
figure amongst the statesmen of that generation. There is
something more modern about him than belongs to his
century. A man of cultivated taste and cosmopolitan
training, he had the contempt of enlightened persons for
the fanaticisms of his times. He was not the man to
suffer persecution, with Baxter, for a creed, or even to
lose his head, with Russell, for a party. Yet if he had not
the faith which animates enthusiasts, he sincerely held
political theories—a fact sufficient to raise him above the
thorough-going cynics of the court of the restoration. His
sense of honour, or the want of robustness in mind and
temperament, kept him aloof from the desperate game in
which the politicians of the day staked their lives, and
threw away their consciences as an incumbrance. Good
fortune threw him into the comparatively safe line of
diplomacy, for which his natural abilities fitted him.
Good fortune, aided by discernment, enabled him to
identify himself with the most respectable achievements
of our foreign policy. He had become famous as the
chief author of the Triple Alliance, and the promoter of
the marriage of William and Mary. He had ventured
far enough into the more troublous element of domestic
politics to invent a highly applauded constitutional device
for smoothing the relations between the crown and Parliament. Like other such devices it went to pieces at the
first contact with realities. Temple retired to cultivate
his garden and write elegant memoirs and essays, and
refused all entreaties to join again in the rough struggles
of the day. Associates, made of sterner stuff, probably

despised him ; but from their own, that is, the selfish
point of view, he was perhaps entitled to laugh last. He
escaped at least with unblemished honour, and enjoyed
the cultivated retirement which statesmen so often profess
to desire, and so seldom achieve. In private, he had
many estimable qualities. He was frank and sensitive ;
he had won diplomatic triumphs by disregarding the
pedantry of official rules ; and he had an equal, though
not an equally intelligent, contempt for the pedantry of
the schools. His style, though often slipshod, often
anticipates the pure and simple English of the Addison
period, and delighted Charles Lamb by its delicate flavour
of aristocratic assumption. He had the vanity of a
" person of quality,"—a lofty, dignified air which became
his flowing periwig, and showed itself in his distinguished features. But in youth, a strong vein of romance
displayed itself in his courtship of Lady Temple, and he
seems to have been correspondingly worshipped by her,
and his sister, Lady Giffard.

The personal friendship of William could not induce
Temple to return to public life. His only son took office,
but soon afterwards killed himself from a morbid sense of
responsibility. Temple retired finally to Moor Park, near
Farnham, in Surrey ; and about the same time received
Swift into his family. Long afterwards, John Temple,
Sir William's nephew, who had quarrelled with Swift,
gave an obviously spiteful account of the terms of this
engagement. Swift, he said, was hired by Sir William
to read to him and be his amanuensis, at the rate of 20*l.*
a year and his board ; but " Sir William never favoured
him with his conversation, nor allowed him to sit down
at table with him." The authority is bad, and we must
be guided by rather precarious inferences in picturing

this important period of Swift's career. The raw Irish
student was probably awkward, and may have been
disagreeable in some matters. Forty years later, we find
from his correspondence with Gay and the Duchess of
Queensberry, that his views as to the distribution of
functions between knives and forks were lamentably
unsettled ; and it is probable that he may in his youth
have been still more heretical as to social conventions.
There were more serious difficulties. The difference which
separated Swift from Temple is not easily measurable.
How can we exaggerate the distance at which a lad, fresh
from college and a remote provincial society, would look
up to the distinguished diplomatist of sixty, who had
been intimate with the two last kings, and was still the
confidential friend of the reigning king, who had been an
actor in the greatest scenes, not only of English, but of
European history, who had been treated with respect by
the ministers of Louis XIV., and in whose honour bells
had been rung, and banquets set forth as he passed
through the great continental cities ? Temple might have
spoken to him, without shocking proprieties, in terms
which, if I may quote the proverbial phrase, would be
offensive " from God Almighty to a blackbeetle."

> Shall I believe a spirit so divine
> Was cast in the same mould with mine ?

is Swift's phrase about Temple, in one of his first
crude poems. We must not infer that circumstances
which would now be offensive to an educated man—the
seat at the second table, the predestined congeniality to
the ladies'-maid of doubtful reputation—would have been
equally offensive then. So long as dependence upon
patrons was a regular incident of the career of a poor

scholar, the corresponding regulations would be taken as
a matter of course. Swift was not necessarily more
degraded by being a dependent of Temple's than Locke
by a similar position in Shaftesbury's family. But it is
true that such a position must always be trying, as many
a governess has felt in more modern days. The position
of the educated dependent must always have had its
specific annoyances. At this period, when the relation
of patron and client was being rapidly modified or
destroyed, the compact would be more than usually
trying to the power of forbearance and mutual kindliness
of the parties concerned. The relation between Sir Roger
de Coverley and the old college friend who became his
chaplain meant good feeling on both sides. When poor
parson Supple became chaplain to Squire Western, and
was liable to be sent back from London to Basingstoke in
search of a forgotten tobacco-box, Supple must have parted
with all self-respect. Swift has incidentally given his
own view of the case in his *Essay on the Fates of Clergy-
men.* It is an application of one of his favourite
doctrines—the advantage possessed by mediocrity over
genius in a world so largely composed of fools. Eugenio,
who represents Jonathan Swift, fails in life because as a
wit and a poet he has not the art of winning patronage.
Corusodes, in whom we have a partial likeness to Tom
Swift, Jonathan's college contemporary, and afterwards
the chaplain of Temple, succeeds by servile respectability.
He never neglected chapel, or lectures : *he* never looked
into a poem : never made a jest himself, or laughed at the
jests of others : but he managed to insinuate himself into
the favour of the noble family where his sister was a
waiting-woman ; shook hands with the butler, taught
the page his catechism ; was sometimes admitted to dine

at the steward's table ; was admitted to read prayers, at
ten shillings a month : and, by winking at his patron's
attentions to his sister, gradually crept into better appointments, married a citizen's widow, and is now fast mounting
towards the top of the ladder ecclesiastical.

Temple was not the man to demand or reward services
so base as those attributed to Corusodes. Nor does it
seem that he would be wanting in the self-respect which
prescribes due courtesy to inferiors, though it admits of a
strict regard for the ceremonial outworks of social dignity.
He would probably neither permit others to take liberties
nor take them himself. If Swift's self-esteem suffered, it
would not be that he objected to offering up the conventional incense, but that he might possibly think that,
after all, the idol was made of rather inferior clay.
Temple, whatever his solid merits, was one of the showiest
statesmen of the time ; but there was no man living with
a keener eye for realities and a more piercing insight into
shams of all kinds than his raw secretary from Ireland.
In later life Swift frequently expressed his scorn for the
mysteries and the "refinements" (to use his favourite
phrase) by which the great men of the world conceal the
low passions and small wisdom actually exerted in affairs
of State. At times he felt that Temple was not merely
claiming the outward show of respect, but setting too high a
value upon his real merits. So when Swift was at the full
flood of fortune, when prime ministers and secretaries of state
were calling him Jonathan, or listening submissively to his
lectures on "whipping-day," he reverts to his early experience. " I often think," he says, when speaking of his own
familiarity with St. John, "what a splutter Sir William
Temple makes about being secretary of state." And
this is a less respectful version of a sentiment expressed a

c

year before, " I am thinking what a veneration we had for
Sir W. Temple because he might have been secretary of
state at fifty, and here is a young fellow hardly thirty in
that employment." In the interval there is another characteristic outburst. " I asked Mr. Secretary (St. John)
what the devil ailed him on Sunday," and warned him
" that I would never be treated like a schoolboy ; that I
had felt too much of that in my life already (meaning Sir
W. Temple) ; that I expected every great minister who
honoured me with his acquaintance, if he heard and saw
anything to my disadvantage, would let me know in plain
words, and not put me in pain to guess by the change or
coldness of his countenance and behaviour." The day
after this effusion, he maintains that he was right in what
he said. " Don't you remember how I used to be in pain
when Sir W. Temple would look cold and out of humour
for three or four days, and I used to suspect a hundred
reasons ? I have plucked up my spirits since then ; faith,
he spoiled a fine gentleman." And yet, if Swift sometimes thought Temple's authority oppressive, he was
ready to admit his substantial merits. Temple, he says,
in his rough marginalia to Burnet's *History*, " was a man
of sense and virtue ;" and the impromptu utterance probably reflects his real feeling.

The year after his first arrival at Temple's, Swift went
back to Ireland by advice of physicians, who " weakly
imagined that his native air might be of some use to recover
his health." It was at this period, we may note in passing,
that Swift began to suffer from a disease which tormented
him through life. Temple sent with him a letter of introduction to Sir Robert Southwell, Secretary of State in
Ireland, which gives an interesting account of their previous relations. Swift said Temple, had lived in his

house, read for him, written for him, and kept his small
accounts. He knew Latin and Greek, and a little French :
wrote a good hand, and was honest and diligent. His
whole family had long been known to Temple, who would
be glad if Southwell would give him a clerkship, or get
him a fellowship in Trinity College. The statement of
Swift's qualifications has now a rather comic sound. An
applicant for a desk in a merchant's office once com-
mended himself, it is said, by the statement that his style
of writing combined scathing sarcasm with the wildest
flights of humour. Swift might have had a better claim
to a place for which such qualities were a recommendation ;
but there is no reason beyond the supposed agreement of
fools to regard genius as a disadvantage in practical life,
to suppose that Swift was deficient in humbler attainments.
Before long, however, he was back at Moor Park ; and a
period followed in which his discontent with the position
probably reached its height. Temple, indeed, must have
discovered that his young dependent was really a man of
capacity. He recommended him to William. In 1692
Swift went to Oxford, to be admitted *ad eundem*, and
received the M.A. degree ; and Swift, writing to thank
his uncle for obtaining the necessary testimonials from
Dublin, adds that he has been most civilly received at
Oxford, on the strength, presumably, of Temple's recommendation, and that he is not to take orders till the king
gives him a prebend. He suspects Temple, however, of
being rather backward in the matter, " because (I suppose) he believes I shall leave him, and (upon some
accounts) he thinks me a little necessary to him." William, it is said, was so far gracious as to offer to make
Swift a captain of horse, and instruct him in the Dutch
mode of cutting asparagus. By this last phrase hangs an

anecdote of later days. Faulkner, the Dublin printer, was dining with Swift, and on asking for a second supply of asparagus, was told by the Dean to finish what he had on his plate. "What, sir, eat my stalks?" "Ay, sir; King William always ate his stalks." "And were you," asked Faulkner's hearer when he related the story, "were you blockhead enough to obey him?" "Yes," replied Faulkner, "and if you had dined with Dean Swift *tête-à-tête* you would have been obliged to eat your stalks too!" For the present Swift was the recipient not the imposer of stalks; and was to receive the first shock, as he tells us, that helped to cure him of his vanity. The question of the Triennial Bill was agitating political personages in the early months of 1693. William and his favourite minister, the Earl of Portland, found their Dutch experience insufficient to guide them in the mysteries of English constitutionalism. Portland came down to consult Temple at Moor Park; and Swift was sent back to explain to the great men that Charles I. had been ruined not by consenting to short Parliaments, but by abandoning the right to dissolve Parliament. Swift says that he was "well versed in English history, though he was under twenty-one years old." (He was really twenty-five, but memory naturally exaggerated his youthfulness). His arguments, however backed by history, failed to carry conviction, and Swift had to unlearn some of the youthful confidence which assumes that reason is the governing force in this world, and that reason means our own opinions. That so young a man should have been employed on such an errand, shows that Temple must have had a good opinion of his capacities; but his want of success, however natural, was felt as a grave discouragement.

That his discontent was growing is clear from other

indications.   Swift's early poems, whatever their defects, have one merit common to all his writings—the merit of a thorough, sometimes an appalling, sincerity.   Two poems which begin to display his real vigour are dated at the end of 1693.   One is an epistle to his schoolfellow, Congreve, expatiating, as some consolation for the cold reception of the *Double Dealer*, upon the contemptible nature of town critics.   Swift describes, as a type of the whole race, a Farnham lad who had left school a year before, and had just returned a " finished spark " from London.

> Stock'd with the latest gibberish of the town.

This wretched little fop came in an evil hour to provoke Swift's hate,—

> My hate, whose lash just heaven has long decreed
> Shall on a day make sin and folly bleed.

And he already applies it with vigour enough to show that with some of the satirist's power he has also the indispensable condition of a considerable accumulation of indignant wrath against the self-appointed arbiters of taste.   The other poem is more remarkable in its personal revelation.   It begins as a congratulation to Temple on his recovery from an illness.   It passes into a description of his own fate, marked by singular bitterness.   He addresses his muse as—

> Malignant Goddess ! bane to my repose,
> Thou universal cause of all my woes.

She is, it seems, a mere delusive meteor, with no real being of her own.   But, if real, why does she persecute him ?

> Wert thou right woman, thou should'st scorn to look
> On an abandon'd wretch by hopes forsook:
> Forsook by hopes, ill fortune's last relief,
> Assign'd for life to unremitting grief ;
> For let heaven's wrath enlarge these weary days
> If hope e'er dawns the smallest of its rays.

And he goes on to declare after some vigorous lines,

> To thee I owe that fatal bent of mind,
> Still to unhappy restless thoughts inclined :
> To thee what oft I vainly strive to hide,
> That scorn of fools, by fools mistook for pride ;
> From thee whatever virtue takes its rise,
> Grows a misfortune, or becomes a vice.

The sudden gush as of bitter waters into the dulcet, insipid current of conventional congratulation, gives additional point to the sentiment. Swift expands the last couplet into a sentiment which remained with him through life. It is a blending of pride and remorse ; a regretful admission of the loftiness of spirit which has caused his misfortunes ; and we are puzzled to say whether the pride or the remorse be the most genuine. For Swift always unites pride and remorse in his consciousness of his own virtues.

The " restlessness " avowed in these verses took the practical form of a rupture with Temple. In his autobiographical fragment he says that he had a scruple of entering into the church merely for support, and Sir William, then being Master of the Rolls in Ireland,[1] offered him an employ of about 120*l.* a year in that office ; whereupon Mr. Swift told him that since he had now an opportunity of living without being driven into

---

[1] Temple had the reversion of his father's office.

the church for a maintenance, he was resolved to go to
Ireland and take holy orders. If the scruple seems rather
finely spun for Swift, the sense of the dignity of his
profession is thoroughly characteristic. Nothing, however,
is more deceptive than our memory of the motives which
directed distant actions. In his contemporary letters there
is no hint of any scruple against preferment in the church,
but a decided objection to insufficient preferment. It is
possible that Swift was confusing dates, and that the
scruple was quieted when he failed to take advantage of
Temple's interest with Southwell. Having declined, he
felt that he had made a free choice of a clerical career. In
1692, as we have seen, he expected a prebend from
Temple's influence with William. But his doubts of
Temple's desire or power to serve him were confirmed.
In June, 1694, he tells a cousin at Lisbon, "I have left
Sir W. Temple a month ago, just as I foretold it you ; and
everything happened exactly as I guessed. He was
extremely angry I left him ; and yet would not oblige
himself any further than upon my good behaviour, nor
would promise anything firmly to me at all ; so that
everybody judged I did best to leave him." He is starting in four days for Dublin, and intends to be ordained
in September. The next letter preserved completes the
story, and implies a painful change in this cavalier tone
of injured pride. Upon going to Dublin, Swift had found
that some recommendation from Temple would be required
by the authorities. He tried to evade the requirement,
but was forced at last to write a letter to Temple, which
nothing but necessity could have extorted. After ex-
plaining the case, he adds, "the particulars expected of
me are what relates to morals and learning, and the
reasons of quitting your honour's family, that is whether

the last was occasioned by any ill actions. They are all
left entirely to your honour's mercy, though in the past
I think I cannot reproach myself any farther than for
infirmities. This," he adds, " is all I dare beg at present
from your honour, under circumstances of life not worth
your regard ;" and all that is left him to wish (" next to
the health and prosperity of your honour's family ") is that
Heaven will show him some day the opportunity of making
his acknowledgments at "your honour's" feet. This
seems to be the only occasion on which we find Swift
confessing to any fault except that of being too virtuous.

The apparent doubt of Temple's magnanimity implied in
the letter was happily not verified. The testimonial seems
to have been sent at once. Swift, in any case, was
ordained deacon on the 28th of October, 1694, and priest
on the 15th of January, 1695. Probably Swift felt that
Temple had behaved with magnanimity, and in any case it
was not very long before he returned to Moor Park. He
had received from Lord Capel, then lord deputy, the small
prebend of Kilroot, worth about 100*l.* a year. Little is
known of his life as a remote country clergyman, except
that he very soon became tired of it.[2] Swift soon
resigned his prebend (in March, 1698) and managed to
obtain the succession for a friend in the neighbourhood.
But before this (in May, 1696) he had returned to Moor
Park. He had grown weary of a life in a remote district,
and Temple had raised his offers. He was glad to be once
more on the edge at least of the great world in which
alone could be found employment worthy of his talents.

-----

[2] It may be noticed in illustration of the growth of the Swift
legend, that two demonstrably false anecdotes—one imputing a
monstrous crime, the other a romantic piece of benevolence to
Swift—refer to this period.

One other incident, indeed, of which a fuller account would be interesting, is connected with this departure. On the eve of his departure, he wrote a passionate letter to "Varina," in plain English Miss Waring, sister of an old college chum. He "solemnly offers to forego all" (all his English prospects, that is) "for her sake." He does not want her fortune; she shall live where she pleases; till he has "pushed his advancement" and is in a position to marry her. The letter is full of true lovers' protestations; reproaches for her coldness; hints at possible causes of jealousies; declarations of the worthlessness of ambition as compared with love; and denunciations of her respect for the little disguises and affected contradictions of her sex, infinitely beneath persons of her pride and his own; paltry maxims calculated only for the "rabble of humanity." "By heaven, Varina," he exclaims, "you are more experienced, and have less virgin innocence than I." The answer must have been unsatisfactory; though from expressions in a letter to his successor to the prebend, we see that the affair was still going on in 1699. It will come to light once more.

Swift was thus at Moor Park in the summer of 1696. He remained till Temple's death in January, 1699. We hear no more of any friction between Swift and his patron; and it seems that the last years of their connexion passed in harmony. Temple was growing old; his wife, after forty years of a happy marriage, had died during Swift's absence in the beginning of 1695; and Temple, though he seems to have been vigorous, and in spite of gout a brisk walker, was approaching the grave. He occupied himself in preparing, with Swift's help, memoirs and letters, which were left to Swift for posthumous publication. Swift's various irritations at Moor Park

have naturally left a stronger impression upon his history
than the quieter hours in which worry and anxiety might
be forgotten in the placid occupations of a country life.
That Swift enjoyed many such hours is tolerably clear.
Moor Park is described by a Swiss traveller who visited
it about 1691,[3] as the "model of an agreeable retreat."
Temple's household was free from the coarse convivialities
of the boozing fox-hunting squires ; whilst the recollection
of its modest neatness made the "magnificent palace" of
Petworth seem pompous and overpowering.   Swift himself remembered the Moor Park gardens, the special pride
of Temple's retirement, with affection, and tried to imitate
them on a small scale in his own garden at Laracor.   Moor
Park is on the edge of the great heaths which stretch
southward to Hindhead, and northwards to Aldershot and
Chobham Ridges.   Though we can scarcely credit him
with a modern taste in scenery, he at least anticipated the
modern faith in athletic exercises.   According to Deane
Swift, he used to run up a hill near Temple's and back
again to his study every two hours, doing the distance of
half a mile in six minutes.   In later life he preached the
duty of walking with admirable perseverance to his
friends.   He joined other exercises occasionally.   "My
Lord," he says to Archbishop King in 1721, "I row after
health like a waterman, and ride after it like a postboy,
and with some little success."   But he had the characteristic
passion of the good and wise for walking.   He mentions
incidentally a walk from Farnham to London, thirty-eight
miles ; and has some association with the Golden Farmer [4]
—a point on the road from which there is still one of the

---

[3] M. Maralt.   See appendix to Courtenay's *Life of Temple*.

[4] The publichouse at the point thus named on the ordnance map
is now (I regret to say) called the Jolly Farmer.

loveliest views in the southern counties, across undulating
breadths of heath and meadow, woodland and down, to
Windsor Forest, St. George's Hill, and the chalk range
from Guildford to Epsom. Perhaps he might have been
a mountaineer in more civilized times ; his poem on the
Carberry rocks seems to indicate a lover of such scenery ;
and he ventured so near the edge of the cliff upon his
stomach, that his servants had to drag him back by his
heels. We find him proposing to walk to Chester at the
rate, I regret to say, of only ten miles a day. In such
rambles, we are told, he used to put up at wayside inns,
where " lodgings for a penny " were advertised ; bribing
the maid with a tester to give him clean sheets and a bed
to himself. The love of the rough humour of waggoners
and hostlers is supposed to have been his inducement to
this practice ; and the refined Orrery associates his coarseness with this lamentable practice ; but amidst the roar
of railways we may think more tolerantly of the humours
of the road in the good old days, when each village had
its humours and traditions and quaint legends, and when
homely maxims of unlettered wisdom were to be picked
up at rustic firesides.

Recreations of this kind were a relief to serious study.
In Temple's library Swift found abundant occupation. " I
am often," he says, in the first period of his residence,
" two or three months without seeing anybody besides
the family." In a later fragment, we find him living
alone " in great state," the cook coming for his orders for
dinner, and the revolutions in the kingdom of the rooks
amusing his leisure. The results of his studies will be
considered directly. A list of books read in 1697 gives
some hint of their general nature. They are chiefly
classical and historical. He read Virgil, Homer, Horace,

Lucretius, Cicero's *Epistles*, Petronius Arbiter, Ælian,
Lucius Florus, Herbert's *Henry VIII.*, Sleidan's *Com-
mentaries, Council of Trent*, Camden's *Elizabeth*, Burnet's
History of the Reformation, Voiture, Blackmore's *Prince
Arthur*, Sir J. Davis's poem of *The Soul*, and two or three
travels, besides Cyprian and Irenæus. We may note the
absence of any theological reading, except in the form of
ecclesiastical history; nor does Swift study philosophy,
of which he seems to have had a sufficient dose in Dublin.
History seems always to have been his favourite study,
and it would naturally have a large part in Temple's
library.

One matter of no small importance to Swift remains to
be mentioned. Temple's family included other dependents besides Swift. The "little parson cousin," Tom
Swift, whom his great relation always mentions with
contempt, became chaplain to Temple. Jonathan's sister
was for some time at Moor Park. But the inmates of the
family most interesting to us were a Rebecca Dingley—
who was in some way related to the family—and Esther
Johnson. Esther Johnson was the daughter of a merchant
of respectable family who died young. Her mother was
known to Lady Giffard, Temple's attached sister; and
after her widowhood, went with her two daughters to live
with the Temples. Mrs. Johnson lived as servant or companion to Lady Giffard for many years after Temple's
death; and little Esther, a remarkably bright and pretty
child, was brought up in the family, and received under
Temple's will a sufficient legacy for her support. It was
of course guessed by a charitable world that she was a
natural child of Sir William's; but there seems to be no
real ground for the hypothesis.[5] She was born, as Swift

[5] The most direct statement to this effect was made in an

tells us, on March 13th, 1681 ; and was therefore a little
over eight when Swift first came to Temple, and fifteen
when he returned from Kilroot.[6] About this age, he
tells us, she got over an infantile delicacy, "grew into
perfect health, and was looked upon as one of the most
beautiful, graceful, and agreeable young women in London.
Her hair was blacker than a raven, and every feature of
her face in perfection." Her conduct and character were
equally remarkable, if we may trust the tutor who taught
her to write, guided her education, and came to regard
her with an affection which was at once the happiness and
the misery of his life.

Temple died January 26, 1699 ; and "with him," said
Swift at the time, "all that was good and amiable among
men." The feeling was doubtless sincere, though Swift,
when moved very deeply, used less conventional phrases.
He was thrown once more upon the world. The expectations
of some settlement in life had not been realized. Temple
had left him 100*l*., the advantage of publishing his posthumous works, which might ultimately bring in 200*l*.
more, and a promise of preferment from the king. Swift
had lived long enough upon the "chameleon's food."
His energies were still running to waste ; and he suffered
the misery of a weakness due, not to want of power but
want of opportunity. His sister writes to a cousin that
her brother had lost his best friend, who had induced
him to give up his Irish preferment by promising prefer-

article in the *Gentleman's Magazine* for 1757. It professes to speak
with authority, but includes such palpable blunders as to carry
little weight.

[6] I am not certain whether this means 1681 or 1681-82. I have
assumed the former date in mentioning Stella's age ; but the other
is equally possible.

ment in England, and had died before the promise had
been fulfilled. Swift was accused of ingratitude by Lord
Palmerston, Temple's nephew, some thirty-five years later.
In reply, he acknowledged an obligation to Temple for
the recommendation to William and the legacy of his
papers; but he adds, "I hope you will not charge my
living in his family as an obligation; for I was educated to
little purpose if I retired to his house for any other motives
than the benefit of his conversation and advice, and the
opportunity of pursuing my studies. For, being born to
no fortune, I was at his death as far to seek as ever; and
perhaps you will allow that I was of some use to him."
Swift seems here to assume that his motives for living
with Temple are necessarily to be estimated by the results
which he obtained. But if he expected more than he
got, he does not suggest any want of goodwill. Temple
had done his best; William's neglect and Temple's death
had made goodwill fruitless. The two might cry quits;
and Swift set to work, not exactly with a sense of injury,
but probably with a strong feeling that a large portion of
his life had been wasted. To Swift, indeed, misfortune
and injury seem equally to have meant resentment,
whether against the fates or some personal object.

One curious document must be noted before considering
the writings which most fully reveal the state of Swift's
mind. In the year 1699 he wrote down some resolutions,
headed "when I come to be old." They are for the most
part pithy and sensible, if it can ever be sensible to make
resolutions for behaviour in a distant future. Swift resolves not to marry a young woman, not to keep young
company unless they desire it, not to repeat stories, not to
listen to knavish, tattling servants, not to be too free of advice, not to brag of former beauty and favour with ladies, to
desire some good friends to inform him when he breaks

these resolutions and to reform accordingly ; and finally, not
to set up for observing all these rules for fear he should
observe none.   These resolutions are not very original in
substance (few resolutions are), though they suggest some
keen observation of his elders ; but one is more remarkable.   " Not to be fond of children, *or let them come near
me hardly.*" The words in italics are blotted out by a later
possessor of the paper, shocked doubtless at the harshness of
the sentiment.   " We do not fortify ourselves with resolutions against what we dislike," says a friendly commen-
tator, " but against what we feel in our weakness we have
reason to believe we are really too much inclined to.''
Yet it is strange that a man should regard the purest and
kindliest of feelings as a weakness to which he is too
much inclined.   No man had stronger affections than
Swift ; no man suffered more agony when they were
wounded ; but in his agony he would commit what to
most men would seem the treason of cursing the affections
instead of simply lamenting the injury, or holding the
affection itself to be its own sufficient reward.   The intense personality of the man reveals itself alternately at
selfishness and as " altruism."   He grappled to his heart
those whom he really loved " as with hoops of steel ;" so
firmly that they became a part of himself ; and that he
considered himself at liberty to regard his love of friends
as he might regard a love of wine, as something to be
regretted when it was too strong for his own happiness.
The attraction was intense ; but implied the absorption
of the weaker nature into his own.   His friendships
were rather annexations than alliances.   The strongest
instance of this characteristic was in his relations to
the charming girl, who must have been in his mind when
he wrote this strange, and unconsciously prophetic,
resolution.

CHAPTER III.

SWIFT came to Temple's house as a raw student. He left
it as the author of one of the most remarkable satires ever
written. His first efforts had been unpromising enough.
Certain *Pindaric Odes*, in which the youthful aspirant
imitated the still popular model of Cowley, are even
comically prosaic. The last of them, dated 1691, is addressed to a queer Athenian Society, promoted by a John
Dunton, a speculative bookseller, whose *Life and Errors* is
still worth a glance from the curious. The Athenian Society was the name of John Dunton himself, and two or three
collaborators who professed in the *Athenian Mercury* to
answer queries ranging over the whole field of human
knowledge. Temple was one of their patrons, and Swift
sent them a panegyrical ode, the merits of which are
sufficiently summed up by Dryden's pithy criticism—
" Cousin Swift, you will never be a poet." Swift disliked
and abused Dryden ever afterwards, though he may have
had better reasons for his enmity than the child's dislike to bitter medicine. Later poems, the *Epistle to
Congreve* and that to Temple already quoted, show
symptoms of growing power and a clearer self-recognition.
In Swift's last residence with Temple, he proved unmis-
takably that he had learnt the secret often so slowly re-

vealed to great writers, the secret of his real strength.
The *Tale of a Tub* was written about 1696 ; part of it
appears to have been seen at Kilroot by his friend, Waring,
Varina's brother; the *Battle of the Books* was written
in 1697. It is a curious proof of Swift's indifference to a
literary reputation that both works remained in manuscript till 1704. The "little parson cousin" Tom Swift,
ventured some kind of claim to a share in the authorship
of the *Tale of a Tub*. Swift treated this claim with the
utmost contempt, but never explicitly claimed for himself
the authorship of what some readers hold to be his most
powerful work.

The *Battle of the Books*, to which we may first attend,
sprang out of the famous controversy as to the relative
merits of the ancients and moderns, which began in France
with Perrault and Fontenelle ; which had been set going
in England by Sir W. Temple's essay upon ancient and
modern learning (1692), and which incidentally led to
the warfare between Bentley and Wotton on one side, and
Boyle and his Oxford allies on the other. A full account
of this celebrated discussion may be found in Professor
Jebb's *Bentley ;* and, as Swift only took the part of a
light skirmisher, nothing more need be said of it in this
place. One point alone is worth notice. The eagerness
of the discussion is characteristic of a time at which the
modern spirit was victoriously revolting against the ancient
canons of taste and philosophy. At first sight, we might
therefore expect the defenders of antiquity to be on the
side of authority. In fact, however, the argument, as
Swift takes it from Temple, is reversed. Temple's theory,
so far as he had any consistent theory, is indicated in the
statement that the moderns gathered "all their learning
from books in the universities." Learning, he suggests,

D

may weaken invention; and people who trust to the
charity of others will always be poor.   Swift accepts and
enforces this doctrine.   The *Battle of the Books* is an
expression of that contempt for pedants which he had
learnt in Dublin, and which is expressed in the ode to the
Athenian Society.   Philosophy, he tells us in that precious
production, "seems to have borrowed some ungrateful
taste of doubts, impertinence, and niceties from every
age through which it passed" (this, I may observe, is verse),
and is now a " medley of all ages," "her face patched over
with modern pedantry."   The moral finds a more poetical
embodiment in the famous apologue of the Bee and the
Spider in the *Battle of the Books*.   The bee had got itself en-
tangled in the spider's web in the library, whilst the books
were beginning to wrangle.   The two have a sharp dispute,
which is summed up by Æsop as arbitrator.   The spider
represents the moderns who spin their scholastic pedantry
out of their own insides ;   whilst the bee, like the ancients,
goes direct to nature.   The moderns produce nothing but
" wrangling and satire, much of a nature with the spider's
poison, which however they pretend to spit wholly out of
themselves is improved by the same arts, by feeding upon
the insects and vermin of the age."   We, the ancients,
"profess to nothing of our own, beyond our wings and our
voice : that is to say, our flights and our language.   For
the rest, whatever we have got has been by infinite labour
and research, and ranging through every corner of nature ;
the difference is that, instead of dirt and poison, we have
rather chosen to fill our hives with honey and wax, thus
furnishing mankind with the two noblest of things, which
are Sweetness and Light."

The Homeric battle which follows is described with
infinite spirit.   Pallas is the patron of the ancients

whilst Momus undertakes the cause of the moderns, and
appeals for help to the malignant deity Criticism, who is
found in her den at the top of a snowy mountain, extended upon the spoils of numberless half-devoured volumes.
By her, as she exclaims in the regulation soliloquy,
children become wiser than their parents, beaux become
politicians, and schoolboys judges of philosophy. She
flies to her darling Wotton, gathering up her person into
an octavo compass; her body grows white and arid and
splits in pieces with dryness; a concoction of gall and
soot is strewn in the shape of letters upon her person;
and so she joins the moderns, "undistinguishable in shape
and dress from the divine Bentley, Wotton's dearest
friend." It is needless to follow the fortunes of the fight
which follows; it is enough to observe that Virgil is
encountered by his translator Dryden in a helmet "nine
times too large for the head, which appeared situate far in
the hinder part, even like the lady in the lobster, or like
a mouse under a canopy of state, or like a shrivelled
beau within the penthouse of a modern periwig, and the
voice was suited to the visage, sounding weak and remote;"
and that the book is concluded by an episode, in which
Bentley and Wotton try a diversion and steal the armour
of Phalaris and Æsop, but are met by Boyle, clad in a
suit of armour given him by all the gods, who transfixes
them on his spear like a brace of woodcocks on an iron
skewer.

The raillery, if taken in its critical aspect, recoils upon
the author. Dryden hardly deserves the scorn of Virgil;
and Bentley, as we know, made short work of Phalaris
and Boyle. But Swift probably knew and cared little for
the merits of the controversy. He expresses his contempt
with characteristic vigour and coarseness; and our pleasure

in his display of exuberant satirical power is not injured by
his obvious misconception of the merits of the case.   The
unflagging spirit of the writing, the fertility and ingenuity of the illustrations, do as much as can be done to
give lasting vitality to what is radically (to my taste at
least) a rather dreary form of wit. The *Battle of the Books*
is the best of the travesties.   Nor in the brilliant assault
upon great names do we at present see anything more
than the buoyant consciousness of power, common in the
unsparing judgments of youth, nor edged as yet by any real
bitterness.   Swift has found out that the world is full of
humbugs ; and goes forth hewing and hacking with super-
abundant energy, not yet aware that he too may conceiv-
ably be a fallible being, and still less that the humbugs
may some day prove too strong for him.

   The same qualities are more conspicuous in the far
greater satire the *Tale of a Tub*. It is so striking a performance that Johnson, who cherished one of his stubborn
prejudices against Swift, doubted whether Swift could
have written it.   " There is in it," he said, " such a vigour
of mind, such a swarm of thoughts, so much of nature,
and art, and life."   The doubt is clearly without the least
foundation, and the estimate upon which it is based is
generally disputed.   The *Tale of a Tub* has certainly not
achieved a reputation equal to that of *Gulliver's Travels*,
to the merits of which Johnson was curiously blind.   Yet
I think that there is this much to be said in favour of
Johnson's theory, namely, that Swift's style reaches its
highest point in the earlier work.   There is less flagging ;
a greater fulness and pressure of energetic thought ; a
power of hitting the nail on the head at the first blow,
which has declined in the work of his maturer years, when
life was weary and thought intermittent.   Swift seems

to have felt this himself. In the twilight of his intellect, he was seen turning over the pages and murmuring to himself, "Good God, what a genius I had when I wrote that book!" In an apology (dated 1709) he makes a statement which may help to explain this fact. "The author," he says, "was then (1696) young, his invention at the height, and his reading fresh in his head. By the assistance of some thinking and much conversation, he had endeavoured to strip himself of as many prejudices as he could." He resolved, as he adds, "to proceed in a manner entirely new;" and he afterwards claims in the most positive terms that through the whole book (including both the tale and the battle of the books) he has not borrowed one "single hint from any writer in the world."[1] No writer has ever been more thoroughly original than Swift, for his writings are simply himself.

The *Tale of a Tub* is another challenge thrown down to pretentious pedantry. The vigorous, self-confident intellect has found out the emptiness and absurdity of a number of the solemn formulæ which pass current in the world, and tears them to pieces with audacious and rejoicing energy. He makes a mock of the paper chains with which solemn professors tried to fetter his activity, and scatters the fragments to the four winds of heaven.

----

[1] Wotton first accused Swift of borrowing the idea of the battle from a French book, by one Coutray, called *Histoire Poétique de la Guerre nouvellement déclarée entre les Anciens et Modernes.* Swift declared (I have no doubt truly) that he had never seen or heard of this book. But Coutray, like Swift, uses the scheme of a mock Homeric battle. The book is prose, but begins with a poem. The resemblance is much closer than Mr. Forster's language would imply; but I agree with him that it does not justify Johnson and Scott in regarding it as more than a natural coincidence. Every detail is different.

In one of the first sections he announces the philosophy afterwards expounded by Herr Teufelsdröckh, according to which "man himself is but a micro-coat;" if one of the suits of clothes called animals "be trimmed up with a gold chain, and a red gown, and a white rod, and a pert look, it is called a Lord Mayor; if certain ermines and furs be placed in a certain position, we style them a judge; and so an apt conjunction of lawn and black satin we entitle a bishop." Though Swift does not himself develop this philosophical doctrine, its later form reflects light upon the earlier theory. For, in truth, Swift's teaching comes to this, that the solemn plausibilities of the world are but so many "shams"—elaborate masks used to disguise the passions, for the most part base and earthly, by which mankind is really impelled. The "digressions" which he introduces with the privilege of a humorist, bear chiefly upon the literary sham. He falls foul of the whole population of Grub Street at starting, and (as I may note in passing) incidentally gives a curious hint of his authorship. He describes himself as a worn-out pamphleteer who has worn his quill to the pith in the service of the State. "Fourscore and eleven pamphlets have I writ under the reigns and for the service of six-and-thirty patrons." Porson first noticed that the same numbers are repeated in *Gulliver's Travels*; Gulliver is fastened with "fourscore and eleven chains" locked to his left leg "with six-and-thirty padlocks." Swift makes the usual onslaught of a young author upon the critics, with more than the usual vigour, and carries on the war against Bentley and his ally by parodying Wotton's remarks upon the ancients. He has discovered many omissions in Homer; "who seems to have read but very superficially either Sendivogus, Behmen, or *Anthroposophia*

Magia." [2] Homer, too, never mentions a saveall; and
has a still worse fault—his "gross ignorance in the
common laws of this realm, and in the doctrine as well as
discipline of the Church of England"—defects, indeed,
for which he has been justly censured by Wotton. Perhaps the most vigorous and certainly the most striking
of these digressions, is that upon "the original use and
improvement of madness in a commonwealth." Just in
passing, as it were, Swift gives the pith of a whole system
of misanthropy, though he as yet seems to be rather indulging a play of fancy, than expressing a settled conviction.
Happiness, he says, is a "perpetual possession of being
well deceived." The wisdom which keeps on the surface
is better than that which persists in officiously prying
into the underlying reality. "Last week I saw a woman
flayed," he observes, "and you will hardly believe how
much it altered her person for the worse." It is best to
be content with patching up the outside, and so assuring
the "serene, peaceful state"—the sublimest point of felicity
—"of being a fool amongst knaves." He goes on to
tell us how useful madmen may be made: how Curtius
may be regarded equally as a madman and a hero for his
leap into the gulf; how the raging, blaspheming, noisy
inmate of Bedlam is fit to have a regiment of dragoons;
and the bustling, sputtering, bawling madman should be
sent to Westminster Hall; and the solemn madman,
dreaming dreams and seeing best in the dark, to preside
over a congregation of dissenters; and how elsewhere you

[2] This was a treatise by Thomas, twin brother of Henry
Vaughan, the "Silurist." It led to a controversy with Henry
More. Vaughan was a Rosicrucian. Swift's contempt for mysteries
is characteristic. Sendivogus was a famous alchemist (1566—
1646).

may find the raw material of the merchant, the courtier, or the monarch. We are all madmen, and happy so far as mad : delusion and peace of mind go together; and the more truth we know, the more shall we recognize that realities are hideous. Swift only plays with his paradoxes. He laughs without troubling himself to decide whether his irony tells against the theories which he ostensibly espouses, or those which he ostensibly attacks. But he has only to adopt in seriousness the fancy with which he is dallying, in order to graduate as a finished pessimist. These, however, are interruptions to the main thread of the book, which is a daring assault upon that serious kind of pedantry which utters itself in theological systems. The three brothers, Peter, Martin, and Jack, represent, as we all know, the Roman Catholic, the Anglican, and the Puritanical varieties of Christianity. They start with a new coat provided for each by their father, and a will to explain the right mode of wearing it; and after some years of faithful observance, they fall in love with the three ladies of wealth, ambition, and pride, get into terribly bad ways and make wild work of the coats and the will. They excuse themselves for wearing shoulder-knots by picking the separate letters S, H, and so forth, out of separate words in the will, and as K is wanting, discover it to be synonymous with C. They reconcile themselves to gold lace by remembering that when they were boys they heard a fellow say that he had heard their father's man say that he would advise his sons to get gold lace when they had money enough to buy it. Then, as the will becomes troublesome in spite of exegetical ingenuity, the eldest brother finds a convenient codicil which can be tacked to it, and will sanction a new fashion of flame-coloured satin. The will expressly forbids silver

fringe on the coats ; but they discover that the word
meaning silver fringe may also signify a broomstick. And
by such devices they go on merrily for a time, till Peter
sets up to be the sole heir and insists upon the obedience
of his brethren. His performances in this position are
trying to their temper. "Whenever it happened that any
rogue of Newgate was condemned to be hanged, Peter
would offer him a pardon for a certain sum of money;
which when the poor caitiff had made all shifts to scrape
up and send, his lordship would return a piece of paper in
this form.

"'To all mayors, sheriffs, jailors, constables, bailiffs,
hangmen, &c. Whereas we are informed that A. B.
remains in the hands of you or some of you, under the
sentence of death : We will and command you, upon sight
hereof to let the said prisoner depart to his own habitation
whether he stands condemned for murder, &c., &c., for
which this shall be your sufficient warrant ; and if you
fail hereof, God damn you and yours to all eternity ; and
so we bid you heartily farewell. Your most humble
man's man, Emperor Peter.'

" The wretches, trusting to this, lost their lives and
their money too." Peter, however, became outrageously
proud. He has been seen to take "three old high-
crowned hats and clap them all on his head three-storey
high, with a huge bunch of keys at his girdle, and
an angling-rod in his hand. In which guise, whoever
went to take him by the hand in the way of salutation,
Peter, with much grace, like a well-educated spaniel, would
present them with his foot ; and if they refused his civility,
then he would raise it as high as their chops, and give
him a damned kick on the mouth, which has ever since
been called a salute."

Peter receives his brothers at dinner, and has nothing
served up but a brown loaf. Come, he says, "fall on
and spare not; here is excellent good mutton," and he
helps them each to a slice. The brothers remonstrate,
and try to point out that they see only bread. They
argue for some time, but have to give in to a conclusive
argument. "'Look ye, gentlemen,' cries Peter in a rage,
'to convince you what a couple of blind, positive, ignorant,
wilful puppies you are, I will use but this simple argument. By G— it is true, good, natural mutton as any
in Leadenhall Market; and G— confound you both
eternally, if you offer to believe otherwise.' Such a
thundering proof as this left no further room for objection;
the two unbelievers began to gather and pocket up their
mistake as hastily as they could," and have to admit besides
that another large dry crust is true juice of the grape.

The brothers Jack and Martin afterwards fall out: and
Jack is treated to a storm of ridicule much in the same
vein as that directed against Peter; and, if less pointed,
certainly not less expressive of contempt. I need not
further follow the details of what Johnson calls this
"wild book," which is in every page brimful of intense
satirical power. I must however say a few words upon a
matter which is of great importance in forming a clear
judgment of Swift's character. The *Tale of a Tub* was
universally attributed to Swift, and led to many doubts of
his orthodoxy and even of his Christianity. Sharpe, Archbishop of York, injured Swift's chances of preferment by
insinuating such doubts to Queen Anne. Swift bitterly
resented the imputation. He prefixed an apology to a
later edition, in which he admitted that he had said some
rash things; but declared that he would forfeit his life if
any one opinion contrary to morality or religion could

be fairly deduced from the book.   He pointed out that he
had attacked no Anglican doctrine.   His ridicule spares
Martin, and is pointed at Peter and Jack.   Like every
satirist who ever wrote, he does not attack the use but the
abuse; and as the Church of England represents for him
the purest embodiment of the truth, an attack upon the
abuses of religion meant an attack upon other churches
only in so far as they diverged from this model.   Critics
have accepted this apology, and treated poor Queen Anne
and her advisers as representing simply the prudery of
the tea-table.   The question, to my thinking, does not
admit of quite so simple an answer.

   If, in fact, we ask what is the true object of Swift's
audacious satire, the answer will depend partly upon our
own estimate of the truth.   Clearly it ridicules "abuses;"
but one man's use is another's abuse : and a dogma may
appear to us venerable or absurd according to our own
creed.   One test, however, may be suggested, which may
guide our decision.   Imagine the *Tale of a Tub* to be read
by Bishop Butler and by Voltaire, who called Swift a
Rabelais perfectionné.   Can any one doubt that the
believer would be scandalized and the scoffer find himself
in a thoroughly congenial element?   Would not any
believer shrink from the use of such weapons even though
directed against his enemies?   Scott urges that the satire
was useful to the high church party because, as he says,
it is important for any institution in Britain (or anywhere
else, we may add) to have the laughers on its side.   But
Scott was too sagacious not to indicate the obvious reply.
The condition of having the laughers on your side is to
be on the side of the laughers.   Advocates of any serious
cause feel that there is a danger in accepting such an
alliance.   The laughers who join you in ridiculing your

enemy, are by no means pledged to refrain from laughing in turn at the laugher. When Swift had ridiculed all the Catholic and all the Puritan dogmas in the most unsparing fashion, could he be sure that the Thirty-nine Articles would escape scot free ? The Catholic theory of a church possessing divine authority, the Puritan theory of a divine voice addressing the individual soul, suggested to him, in their concrete embodiments at least, nothing but a horselaugh. Could any one be sure that the Anglican embodiment of the same theories might not be turned to equal account by the scoffer ? Was the true bearing of Swift's satire in fact limited to the deviations from sound Church of England doctrine, or might it not be directed against the very vital principle of the doctrine itself ?

Swift's blindness to such criticisms was thoroughly characteristic. He professes, as we have seen, that he had need to clear his mind of *real* prejudices. He admits that the process might be pushed too far; that is, that in abandoning a prejudice you may be losing a principle. In fact, the prejudices from which Swift had sought to free himself —and no doubt with great success—were the prejudices of other people. For them he felt unlimited contempt. But the prejudice which had grown up in his mind, strengthened with his strength, and become intertwined with all his personal affections and antipathies, was no longer a prejudice in his eyes, but a sacred principle. The intensity of his contempt for the follies of others shut his eyes effectually to any similarity between their tenets and his own. His principles, true or false, were prejudices in the highest degree, if by a prejudice we mean an opinion cherished because it has somehow or other become ours, though the "somehow" may exclude all reference to

reason. Swift never troubled himself to assign any
philosophical basis for his doctrines ; having, indeed, a
hearty contempt for philosophizing in general. He clung
to the doctrines of his church, not because he could give
abstract reasons for his belief, but simply because the
church happened to be his. It is equally true of all his
creeds, political or theological, that he loved them as he
loved his friends, simply because they had become a part
of himself, and were therefore identified with all his
hopes, ambitions, and aspirations public or private. We
shall see hereafter how fiercely he attacked the dissenters,
and how scornfully he repudiated all arguments founded
upon the desirability of union amongst Protestants. To
a calm outside observer differences might appear to be
superficial ; but to him, no difference could be other than
radical and profound which in fact divided him from an
antagonist. In attacking the Presbyterians, cried more
temperate people, you are attacking your brothers and
your own opinions. No, replied Swift, I am attacking
the corruption of my principles ; hideous caricatures of
myself ; caricatures the more hateful in proportion to their
apparent likeness. And therefore, whether in political or
theological warfare, he was sublimely unconscious of the
possible reaction of his arguments.

Swift took a characteristic mode of showing that if upon
some points he accidentally agreed with the unbeliever,
it was not from any covert sympathy. Two of his most
vigorous pieces of satire in later days are directed against
the deists. In 1708 he published an *Argument to prove
that the abolishing of Christianity in England may, as
things now stand, be attended with some inconveniences,
and perhaps not produce those many good effects proposed
thereby.* And in 1713, in the midst of his most eager

political warfare, he published *Mr. Collins's Discourse of
Freethinking, put into plain English, by way of abstract,
for use of the poor.* No one who reads these pamphlets
can deny that the keenest satire may be directed against
infidels as well as against Christians. The last is an
admirable parody, in which poor Collins's arguments are
turned against himself with ingenious and provoking irony.
The first is perhaps Swift's cleverest application of the
same method. A nominal religion, he urges gravely, is of
some use, for if men cannot be allowed a God to revile or
renounce, they will speak evil of dignities, and may even
come to "reflect upon the ministry." If Christianity
were once abolished, the wits would be deprivèd of their
favourite topic. "Who would ever have suspected Asgil
for a wit or Toland for a philosopher if the inexhaustible
stock of Christianity had not been at hand to provide
them with materials?" The abolition of Christianity
moreover may possibly bring the Church into danger, for
atheists, deists, and Socinians have little zeal for the present
ecclesiastical establishment ; and if they once get rid of
Christianity, they may aim at setting up Presbyterianism.
Moreover, as long as we keep to any religion, we do not
strike at the root of the evil. The freethinkers consider
that all the parts hold together, and that if you pull out
one nail the whole fabric will fall. Which, he says,
was happily expressed by one who heard that a text brought
in proof of the Trinity, was differently read in some
ancient manuscript ; whereupon he suddenly leaped
through a long *sorites* to the logical conclusion : "Why,
if it be as you say, I may safely . . . . drink on and
defy the parson."

A serious meaning underlies Swift's sarcasms.
Collins had argued in defence of the greatest possible

freedom of discussion ; and tacitly assumed that such discussion would lead to disbelief of Christianity. Opponents of the liberal school had answered by claiming his first principle as their own. They argued that religion was based upon reason, and would be strengthened instead of weakened by free inquiry. Swift virtually takes a different position. He objects to freethinking because ordinary minds are totally unfit for such inquiries. "The bulk of mankind," as he puts it, is as "well qualified for flying as thinking ;" and therefore free-thought would lead to anarchy, atheism, and immorality, as liberty to fly would lead to a breaking of necks.

Collins rails at priests as tyrants upheld by imposture. Swift virtually replies that they are the sole guides to truth and guardians of morality, and that theology should be left to them, as medicine to physicians and law to lawyers. The argument against the abolition of Christianity takes the same ground. Religion, however little regard is paid to it in practice, is in fact the one great security for a decent degree of social order ; and the rash fools who venture to reject what they do not understand, are public enemies as well as ignorant sciolists.

The same view is taken in Swift's sermons. He said of himself that he could only preach political pamphlets. Several of the twelve sermons preserved are in fact directly aimed at some of the political and social grievances which he was habitually denouncing. If not exactly "pamphlets," they are sermons in aid of pamphlets. Others are vigorous and sincere moral discourses. One alone deals with a purely theological topic : the doctrine of the Trinity. His view is simply that "men of wicked lives would be very glad if there were no truth in Christianity at all." They therefore cavil at the mysteries to find some

excuse for giving up the whole. He replies in effect that
there must be mystery though not contradiction, everywhere,
and that if we do not accept humbly what is taught in
the Scriptures, we must give up Christianity, and con-
sequently, as he holds, all moral obligation, at once. The
cavil is merely the pretext of an evil conscience. Swift's
religion thus partook of the directly practical nature of
his whole character. He was absolutely indifferent to
speculative philosophy. He was even more indifferent to
the mystical or imaginative aspects of religion. He loved
downright concrete realities, and was not the man to lose
himself in an *Oh, altitudo !* or in any train of thought or
emotion not directly bearing upon the actual business of
the world. Though no man had more pride in his order
or love of its privileges, Swift never emphasized his professional character. He wished to be accepted as a man of
the world and of business. He despised the unpractical
and visionary type, and the kind of religious utterance
congenial to men of that type was abhorrent to him. He
shrank invariably too from any display of his emotion, and
would have felt the heartiest contempt for the sentimentalism of his day. At once the proudest and most
sensitive of men, it was his imperative instinct to hide
his emotions as much as possible. In cases of great
excitement, he retired into some secluded corner, where,
if he was forced to feel, he could be sure of hiding his
feelings. He always masks his strongest passions under
some ironical veil, and thus practised what his friends
regarded as an inverted hypocrisy. Delany tells us that
he stayed for six months in Swift's house, before discovering that the dean always read prayers to his servants at a
fixed hour in private. A deep feeling of solemnity showed
itself in his manner of performing public religious exercises,

but Delany, a man of a very different temperament, blames his friend for carrying his reserve in all such matters to extremes. In certain respects Swift was ostentatious enough ; but this intense dislike to wearing his heart upon his sleeve, to laying bare the secrets of his affections before unsympathetic eyes, is one of his most indelible characteristics. Swift could never have felt the slightest sympathy for the kind of preacher who courts applause by a public exhibition of intimate joys and sorrows ; and was less afraid of suppressing some genuine emotion than of showing any in the slightest degree unreal.

Although Swift took in the main what may be called the political view of religion, he did not by any means accept that view in its cynical form. He did not, that is, hold, in Gibbon's famous phrase, that all religions were equally false and equally useful. His religious instincts were as strong and genuine as they were markedly undemonstrative. He came to take (I am anticipating a little) a gloomy view of the world and of human nature. He had the most settled conviction not only of the misery of human life but of the feebleness of the good elements in the world. The bad and the stupid are the best fitted for life, as we find it. Virtue is generally a misfortune ; the more we sympathize, the more cause we have for wretchedness ; our affections give us the purest kind of happiness, and yet our affections expose us to sufferings which more than outweigh the enjoyments. There is no such thing, he said in his decline, as " a fine old gentleman ;" if so and so had had either a mind or a body worth a farthing," they would have worn him out long ago." That became a typical sentiment with Swift. His doctrine was, briefly, that : virtue was the one thing which

E

deserved love and admiration ; and yet that virtue in
this hideous chaos of a world, involved misery and decay.
What would be the logical result of such a creed, I do
not presume to say.   Certainly, we should guess, something more pessimistic or Manichæan than suits the
ordinary interpretation of Christian doctrine.   But for
Swift this state of mind carried with it the necessity of
clinging to some religious creed: not because the creed held
out promises of a better hereafter, for Swift was too much
absorbed in the present to dwell much upon such beliefs ;
but rather because it provided him with some sort of
fixed convictions in this strange and disastrous muddle.
If it did not give a solution in terms intelligible to the
human intellect, it encouraged the belief that some
solution existed.   It justified him to himself for continuing to respect morality, and for going on living, when
all the game of life seemed to be decidedly going in favour
of the devil, and suicide to be the most reasonable course.
At least, it enabled him to associate himself with the
causes and principles which he recognized as the most
ennobling element in the world's "mad farce ;" and to
utter himself in formulæ consecrated by the use of such
wise and good beings as had hitherto shown themselves
amongst a wretched race.   Placed in another situation,
Swift no doubt might have put his creed—to speak after
the Clothes Philosophy—into a different dress.   The substance could not have been altered, unless his whole
character as well as his particular opinions had been
profoundly modified.

CHAPTER IV.

SWIFT at the age of thirty-one had gained a small amount of cash, and a promise from William. He applied to the king, but the great man ·in whom he trusted failed to deliver his petition ; and, after some delay, he accepted an invitation to become chaplain and secretary to the Earl of Berkeley, just made one of the Lords Justices of Ireland. He acted as secretary on the journey to Ireland : but upon reaching Dublin, Lord Berkeley gave the post to another man, who had persuaded him that it was unfit for a clergyman. Swift next claimed the deanery of Derry, which soon became vacant. The secretary had been bribed by 1000*l.* from another candidate, upon whom the deanery was bestowed : but Swift was told that he might still have the preference for an equal bribe. Unable or unwilling to comply, he took leave of Berkeley and the secretary, with the pithy remark, "God confound you both for a couple of scoundrels." He was partly pacified, however (February 1700), by the gift of Laracor, a village near Trim, some twenty miles from Dublin. Two other small livings, and a prebend in the cathedral of St. Patrick, made up a revenue of about 230*l.* a year.[1] The income enabled him to live ; but, in spite of the

---

[1] See Forster, p. 117.

rigid economy which he always practised, did not enable
him to save. Marriage under such circumstances would
have meant the abandonment of an ambitious career. A
wife and family would have anchored him to his country
parsonage.

This may help to explain an unpleasant episode which
followed. Poor Varina had resisted Swift's entreaties,
on the ground of her own ill-health and Swift's want of
fortune. She now, it seems, thought that the economical
difficulty was removed by Swift's preferment, and wished
the marriage to take place. Swift replied in a letter,
which contains all our information : and to which I
can apply no other epithet than brutal. Some men
might feel bound to fulfil a marriage engagement, even
when love had grown cold ; others might think it better
to break it off in the interests of both parties. Swift's
plan was to offer to fulfil it on conditions so insulting
that no one with a grain of self-respect could accept. In
his letter he expresses resentment for Miss Waring's previous treatment of him ; he reproaches her bitterly with
the company in which she lives—including, as it seems,
her mother ; no young woman in the world with her
income should " dwindle away her health in such a sink
and among such family conversation." He explains that
he is still poor ; he doubts the improvement of her own
health ; and he then says that if she will submit to be
educated so as to be capable of entertaining him : to
accept all his likes and dislikes : to soothe his ill-humour,
and live cheerfully wherever he pleases : he will take
her without inquiring into her looks or her income.
" Cleanliness in the first, and competency in the other, is
all I look for." Swift could be the most persistent and
ardent of friends. But, when any one tried to enforce

claims no longer congenial to his feelings, the appeal to
the galling obligation stung him into ferocity, and brought
out the most brutal side of his imperious nature.

It was in the course of the next year that Swift took a
step which has sometimes been associated with this. The
death of Temple had left Esther Johnson homeless. The
small fortune left to her by Temple consisted of an Irish
farm. Swift suggested to her that she and her friend
Mrs. Dingley would get better interest for their money,
and live more cheaply in Ireland than in England. This
change of abode naturally made people talk. The little
parson cousin asked (in 1706) whether Jonathan had been
able to resist the charms of the two ladies who had
marched from Moor Park to Dublin " with full resolution
to engage him." Swift was now (1701) in his thirty-fourth
year, and Stella a singularly beautiful and attractive girl
of twenty. The anomalous connexion was close, and yet
most carefully guarded against scandal. In Swift's
absence, the ladies occupied his apartments at Dublin.
When he and they were in the same place they took separate
lodgings. Twice, it seems, they accompanied him on visits to
England. But Swift never saw Esther Johnson except in
presence of a third person; and he incidentally declares in
1726—near the end of her life—that he had not seen her
in a morning " these dozen years, except once or twice in a
journey." The relations thus regulated remained unaltered
for several years to come. Swift's duties at Laracor were not
excessive. He reckons his congregation at fifteen persons,
" most of them gentle and all simple." He gave notice,
says Orrery, that he would read prayers every Wednesday
and Friday. The congregation on the first Wednesday
consisted of himself and his clerk, and Swift began the
service, " Dearly beloved Roger, the scripture moveth you

and me," and so forth.   This being attributed to Swift, is
supposed to be an exquisite piece of facetiousness; but
we may hope that, as Scott gives us reason to think, it
was really one of the drifting jests that stuck for a time
to the skirts of the famous humorist.   What is certain
is, that Swift did his best, with narrow means, to improve
the living—rebuilt the house, laid out the garden, increased
the glebe from one acre to twenty, and endowed the living
with tithes bought by himself.   He left the tithes on the
remarkable condition (suggested probably by his fears of
Presbyterian ascendancy) that, if another form of Christian
religion should become the established faith in this kingdom, they should go to the poor—excluding Jews, Atheists,
and infidels.   Swift became attached to Laracor, and the
gardens which he planted in humble imitation of Moor
Park; he made friends of some of the neighbours;
though he detested Trim, where "the people were as great
rascals as the gentlemen;" but Laracor was rather an
occasional retreat than a centre of his interests.   During the
following years Swift was often at the castle at Dublin,
and passed considerable periods in London, leaving a
curate in charge of the minute congregation at Laracor.

He kept upon friendly terms with successive Viceroys.
He had, as we have seen, extorted a partial concession of
his claims from Lord Berkeley.   For Lord Berkeley, if
we may argue from a very gross lampoon, he can have felt
nothing but contempt.   But he had a high respect for
Lady Berkeley; and one of the daughters, afterwards
Lady Betty Germaine, a very sensible and kindly woman,
retained his friendship through life, and in letters written
long afterwards refers with evident fondness to the old days
of familiarity.   He was intimate, again, with the family
of the Duke of Ormond, who became Lord Lieutenant in

1703, and, again, was the close friend of one of the daughters. He was deeply grieved by her death a few years later, soon after her marriage to Lord Ashburnham. "I hate life," he says characteristically, "when I think it exposed to such accidents; and to see so many thousand wretches burdening the earth when such as her die, makes me think God did never intend life for a blessing." When Lord Pembroke succeeded Ormond, Swift still continued chaplain, and carried on a queer commerce of punning with Pembroke. It is the first indication of a habit which lasted, as we shall see, through life. One might be tempted to say, were it not for the conclusive evidence to the contrary, that this love of the most mechanical variety of facetiousness implied an absence of any true sense of humour. Swift, indeed, was giving proofs that he possessed a full share of that ambiguous talent. It would be difficult to find a more perfect performance of its kind than the poem by which he amused the Berkeley family in 1700. It is the *Petition of Mrs. Frances Harris*, a chambermaid, who had lost her purse, and whose peculiar style of language, as well as the unsympathetic comments of her various fellow-servants, are preserved with extraordinary felicity in a peculiar doggerel invented for the purpose by Swift. One fancies that the famous Mrs. Harris of Mrs. Gamp's reminiscences was a phantasmal descendant of Swift's heroine. He lays bare the workings of the menial intellect with the clearness of a master.

Neither Laracor nor Dublin could keep Swift from London.[2] During the ten years succeeding 1700, he must

[2] He was in England from April to September in 1701, from April to November in 1702, from November 1703 till May 1704, for an uncertain part of 1705, and again for over fifteen months from the end of 1707 till the beginning of 1709.

have passed over four in England. In the last period
mentioned he was acting as an agent for the Church of
Ir land. In the others he was attracted by pleasure or
ambition. He had already many introductions to London
society, through Temple, through the Irish Viceroys, and
through Congreve, the most famous of then living wits.
A successful pamphlet, to be presently mentioned, helped
his rise to fame. London society was easy of access
for a man of Swift's qualities. The divisions of rank
were doubtless more strongly marked than now. Yet
society was relatively so small, and concentrated in so
small a space, that admission into the upper circle meant
an easy introduction to every one worth knowing. Any
noticeable person became, as it were, member of a club
which had a tacit existence, though there was no
single place of meeting or recognized organization. Swift
soon became known at the coffee-houses, which have been
superseded by the clubs of modern times. At one time,
according to a story vague as to dates, he got the name
of the "mad parson" from Addison and others, by his
habit of taking half-an-hour's smart walk to and fro in
the coffee-house, and then departing in silence. At last
he abruptly accosted a stranger from the country:
"Pray, sir, do you remember any good weather in the
world?" "Yes, sir," was the reply, "I thank God I
remember a great deal of good weather in my time."
"That," said Swift, "is more than I can say. I never
remember any weather that was not too hot, or too cold,
or too wet, or too dry : but, however God Almighty con-
trives it, at the end of the year 'tis all very well;" with
which sentiment he vanished. Whatever his introduction
Swift would soon make himself felt. The *Tale of a Tub*
appeared—with a very complimentary dedication to

Somers—in 1704, and revealed powers beyond the
rivalry of any living author.

In the year 1705 Swift became intimate with Addison,
who wrote in a copy of his *Travels in Italy*, To *Jonathan Swift, the most agreeable companion, the truest
friend, and the greatest genius of his age, this work is presented by his most humble servant the author*. Though
the word "genius" had scarcely its present strength of
meaning, the phrase certainly implies that Addison knew
Swift's authorship of the *Tale*, and with all his decorum
was not repelled by its audacious satire. The pair
formed a close friendship, which is honourable to both.
For it proves that if Swift was imperious and Addison a
little too fond of the adulation of "wits and Templars,"
each could enjoy the society of an intellectual equal. They
met, we may fancy, like absolute kings, accustomed to the
incense of courtiers, and not inaccessible to its charms ; and
yet glad at times to throw aside state and associate with
each other without jealousy. Addison, we know, was
most charming when talking to a single companion, and
Delany repeats Swift's statement that, often as they spent
their evenings together, they never wished for a third.
Steele, for a time, was joined in what Swift calls a triumvirate ; and though political strife led to a complete breach
with Steele and a temporary eclipse of familiarity with
Addison, it never diminished Swift's affection for his great
rival. "That man," he said once, "has virtue enough
to give reputation to an age," and the phrase expresses his
settled opinion. Swift, however, had a low opinion of
the society of the average "wit." "The worst conversation I ever heard in my life," he says, "was that at
Wills' coffee-house, where the wits (as they were called)
used formerly to assemble ;" and he speaks with a con-

tempt recalling Pope's satire upon the "little senate," of
the absurd self-importance and the foolish adulation of
the students and Templars who listened to these oracles.
Others have suspected that many famous coteries of which
literary people are accustomed to speak with unction, probably fell as far short in reality of their traditional pleasant-
ness. Swift's friendship with Addison was partly due,
we may fancy, to the difference in temper and talent
which fitted each to be complement of the other. A
curious proof of the mutual goodwill is given by the history
of Swift's *Baucis and Philemon*. It is a humorous and
agreeable enough travesty of Ovid ; a bit of good-humoured
pleasantry, which we may take as it was intended. The
performance was in the spirit of the time, and if Swift
had not the lightness of touch of his contemporaries, Prior,
Gay, Parnell, and Pope, he perhaps makes up for it by
greater force and directness. But the piece is mainly
remarkable because, as he tells us, Addison made him
"blot out four score lines, add four score, and alter four
score," though the whole consisted of only 178 verses.[3]
Swift showed a complete absence of the ordinary touchi-
ness of authors. His indifference to literary fame as
to its pecuniary rewards, was conspicuous. He was too
proud, as he truly said, to be vain. His sense of dignity
restrained him from petty sensibility. When a clergyman
regretted some emendations which had been hastily suggested by himself and accepted by Swift, Swift replied
that it mattered little, and that he would not give grounds
by adhering to his own opinion, for an imputation of

---

[3] Mr. Forster found the original MS., and gives us the exact
numbers : 96 omitted, 44 added, 22 altered. The whole was 178
lines *after* the omissions.

vanity. If Swift was egotistical, there was nothing petty even in his egotism.

A piece of facetiousness, started by Swift in the last of his visits to London, has become famous. A cobbler called Partridge had set up as an astrologer, and published predictions in the style of *Zadkiel's Almanac*. Swift amused himself in the beginning of 1708 by publishing a rival prediction under the name of Isaac Bickerstaff. Bickerstaff professed that he would give verifiable and definite predictions, instead of the vague oracular utterances of his rival. The first of these predictions announced the approaching death, at 11 p.m., on March 29th, of Partridge himself. Directly after that day appeared a letter " to a person of honour," announcing the fulfilment of the prediction by the death of Partridge within four hours of the date assigned. Partridge took up the matter seriously, and indignantly declared himself, in a new Almanac, to be alive. Bickerstaff retorted in a humorous Vindication, arguing that Partridge was really dead ; that his continuing to write almanacs was no proof to the contrary, and so forth. All the wits, great and small, took part in the joke : the Portuguese inquisition, so it is said, were sufficiently taken in to condemn Bickerstaff to the flames ; and Steele, who started the *Tatler*, whilst the joke was afoot, adopted the name of Bickerstaff for the imaginary author. Dutiful biographers agree to admire this as a wonderful piece of fun. The joke does not strike me, I will confess, as of very exquisite flavour ; but it is a curious illustration of a peculiarity to which Swift owed some of his power, and which seems to have suggested many of the mythical anecdotes about him. His humour very easily took the form of practical joking. In those days, the mutual understanding of the little clique of wits made it easy to

get a hoax taken up by the whole body. They joined to
persecute poor Partridge, as the undergraduates at a
modern college might join to tease some obnoxious
tradesman. Swift's peculiar irony fitted him to take
the lead ; for it implied a singular pleasure in realizing
the minute consequences of some given hypothesis, and
working out in detail some grotesque or striking theory.
The love of practical jokes, which seems to have accompanied him through life, is one of the less edifying
manifestations of the tendency. It seems as if he could
not quite enjoy a jest till it was translated into actual
tangible fact. The fancy does not suffice him till it is
realized. If the story about "dearly beloved Roger" be
true, it is a case in point. Sydney Smith would have
been content with suggesting that such a thing might be
done. Swift was not satisfied till he had done it. And
even if it be not true, it has been accepted because it is
like the truth. We could almost fancy that if Swift had
thought of Charles Lamb's famous quibble about walking
on an empty stomach ("on whose empty stomach ?"), he
would have liked to carry it out by an actual promenade
on real human flesh and blood.

Swift became intimate with Irish viceroys, and with
the most famous wits and statesmen of London. But
he received none of the good things bestowed so freely
upon contemporary men of letters. In 1705, Addison,
his intimate friend, and his junior by five years, had
sprung from a garret to a comfortable office. Other men
passed Swift in the race. He notes significantly in 1708,
that "a young fellow," a friend of his, had just received
a sinecure of 400l. a year, as an addition to another of
300l. Towards the end of 1704 he had already complained that he got "nothing but the good words and
wishes of a decayed ministry, whose lives and mine will

probably wear out before they can serve either my little
hopes, or their own ambition." Swift still remained in
his own district, " a hedge-parson," flattered, caressed and
neglected. And yet he held,[4] that it was easier to provide
for ten men in the church, than for one in a civil employment. To understand his claims, and the modes by
which he used to enforce them, we must advert briefly to
the state of English politics. A clear apprehension of
Swift's relation to the ministers of the day is essential to
any satisfactory estimate of his career.

The reign of Queen Anne was a period of violent party
spirit. At the end of 1703, Swift humorously declares
that even the cats and dogs were infected with the Whig
and Tory animosity. The "very ladies" were divided into
high church and low ; and, " out of zeal for religion, had
hardly time to say their prayers." The gentle satire of
Addison and Steele, in the *Spectator*, confirms Swift's
contemporary lamentations, as to the baneful effects of
party zeal upon private friendship. And yet, it has been
often said, that the party issues were hopelessly confounded. Lord Stanhope argues—and he is only repeating
what Swift frequently said—that Whigs and Tories had
exchanged principles.[5] In later years, Swift constantly
asserted that he attacked the Whigs in defence of the
true Whig faith. He belonged indeed to a party, almost
limited to himself : for he avowed himself to be the
anomalous hybrid, a High-church Whig. We must therefore inquire a little further into the true meaning of the
accepted shibboleths.

Swift had come from Ireland, saturated with the pre-

[4] See letter to *Peterborough*, May 6, 1711.
[5] In most of their principles the two parties seem to have
shifted opinions since their institution in the reign of Charles II.
Examiner, No. 43. May 31, 1711.

prejudices of his caste. The highest Tory in Ireland, as
he told William, would make a tolerable Whig in
England. For the English colonists in Ireland, the ex-
pulsion of James was a condition not of party success
but of existence. Swift, whose personal and family
interests were identified with those of the English in
Ireland, could repudiate James with his whole heart, and
heartily accepted the revolution ; he was therefore a
Whig, so far as attachment to " revolution principles "
was the distinctive badge of Whiggism. Swift despised
James, and he hated Popery from first to last. Contempt and hatred with him were never equivocal, and in
this case they sprang as much from his energetic sense as
from his early prejudices. Jacobitism was becoming a
sham, and therefore offensive to men of insight into facts.
Its ghost walked the earth for some time longer, and at
times aped reality ; but it meant mere sentimentalism
or vague discontent. Swift, when asked to explain its
persistence, said that when he was in pain and lying on
his right side, he naturally turned to his left, though he
might have no prospect of benefit from the change.[6]
The country squire, who drank healths to the king over
the water, was tired of the Georges, and shared the fears
of the typical Western, that his lands were in danger of
being sent to Hanover. The Stuarts had been in exile
long enough to win the love of some of their subjects.
Sufficient time had elapsed to erase from short memories
the true cause of their fall. Squires and parsons did not
cherish less warmly the privileges in defence of which
they had sent the last Stuart king about his business.
Rather the privileges had become so much a matter of

[6] Delany, p. 211.

course that the very fear of any assault seemed visionary. The Jacobitism of later days did not mean any discontent with revolution principles, but dislike to the revolution dynasty. The Whig indeed argued with true party logic, that every Tory must be a Jacobite, and every Jacobite a lover of arbitrary rule. In truth a man might wish to restore the Stuarts without wishing to restore the principles for which the Stuarts had been expelled : he might be a Jacobite without being a lover of arbitrary rule ; and still more easily might he be a Tory without being a Jacobite. Swift constantly asserted—and in a sense with perfect truth—that the revolution had been carried out in defence of the Church of England, and chiefly by attached members of the Church. To be a sound churchman was, so far, to be pledged against the family which had assailed the Church.

Swift's Whiggism would naturally be strengthened by his personal relation with Temple, and with various Whigs whom he came to know through Temple. But Swift, I have said, was a churchman as well as a Whig ; as staunch a churchman as Laud, and as ready, I imagine, to have gone to the block or to prison in defence of his church as any one from the days of Laud to those of Mr. Green. For a time his zeal was not called into play ; the war absorbed all interests. Marlborough and Godolphin, the great heads of the family clique which dominated poor Queen Anne, had begun as Tories and churchmen, supported by a Tory majority. The war had been dictated by a national sentiment : but from the beginning it was really a Whig war : for it was a war against Louis,Popery, and the Pretender. And thus, the great men who were identified with the war, began slowly to edge over to the party whose principles were

the war principles; who hated the Pope, the Pretender,
and the King of France, as their ancestors had hated
Phillip of Spain, or as their descendants hated Napoleon.
The war meant alliance with the Dutch, who had been
the martyrs, and were the enthusiastic defenders of tole-
ration and free thought; and it forced English ministers,
almost in spite of themselves, into the most successful
piece of statesmanship of the century, the Union with
Scotland.   Now Swift hated the Dutch and hated the
Scotch, with a vehemence that becomes almost ludicrous.
The margin of his Burnet was scribbled over with
execrations against the Scots.   " Most damnable Scots,"
" Scots hell-hounds," " Scotch dogs," " cursed Scots
still," " hellish Scottish dogs," are a few of his spontaneous flowers of speech.   His prejudices are the
prejudices of his class intensified as all passions were
intensified in him.   Swift regarded Scotchmen as the
most virulent and dangerous of all dissenters; they were
represented to him by the Irish Presbyterians, the
natural rivals of his church.   He reviled the Union,
because it implied the recognition by the State of a sect
which regarded the Church of England as little better
than a manifestation of Antichrist.   And, in this sense,
Swift's sympathies were with the Tories.   For in truth
the real contrast between Whigs and Tories, in respect
of which there is a perfect continuity of principle,
depended upon the fact that the Whigs reflected the
sentiments of the middle classes, the " monied men "
and the dissenters; whilst the Tories reflected the sentiments of the land and the church.   Each party might
occasionally adopt the commonplaces or accept the
measures generally associated with its antagonists;
but at bottom, the distinction was between squire

and parson on one side, tradesmen and banker on the other.

The domestic politics of the reign of Anne turned upon this difference. The history is a history of the gradual shifting of government to the Whig side, and the growing alienation of the clergy and squires, accelerated by a system which caused the fiscal burden of the war to fall chiefly upon the land. Bearing this in mind, Swift's conduct is perfectly intelligible. His first plunge into politics was in 1701. Poor King William was in the thick of the perplexities caused by the mysterious perverseness of English politicians. The king's ministers, supported by the House of Lords, had lost the command of the House of Commons. It had not yet come to be understood that the Cabinet was to be a mere committee of the House of Commons. The personal wishes of the sovereign, and the alliances and jealousies of great courtiers, were still highly important factors in the political situation; as indeed both the composition and the subsequent behaviour of the Commons could be controlled to a considerable extent by legitimate and other influences of the Crown. The Commons, unable to make their will obeyed, proceeded to impeach Somers and other ministers. A bitter struggle took place between the two Houses, which was suspended by the summer recess. At this crisis Swift published his *Discourse on the Dissensions in Athens and Rome.* The abstract political argument is as good or as bad as nine hundred and ninety-nine out of a thousand political treatises—that is to say, a repetition of familiar commonplaces ; and the mode of applying precedents from ancient politics would now strike us as pedantic. The pamphlet, however, is dignified and well-written, and the application to the immediate difficulty is pointed. His

F

argument is, briefly, that the House of Commons is showing a factious, tyrannical temper, identical in its nature
with that of a single tyrant and as dangerous in its consequences, that it has therefore ceased to reflect the
opinions of its constituents, and has endangered the
sacred balance between the three primary elements of our
constitution, upon which its safe working depends.

The pamphlet was from beginning to end a remonstrance against the impeachments, and therefore a defence
of the Whig lords ; for whom sufficiently satisfactory
parallels are vaguely indicated in Pericles, Aristides, and
so forth.   It was " greedily bought ;" it was attributed to
Somers and to the great Whig bishop, Burnet, who had
to disown it for fear of an impeachment.   An Irish bishop,
it is said, called Swift a " very positive young man " for
doubting Burnet's authorship; whereupon Swift had to
claim it for himself.   Youthful vanity, according to his own
account, induced him to make the admission, which would
certainly not have been withheld by adult discretion.
For the result was that Somers, Halifax, and Sunderland,
three of the great Whig junto, took him up, often admitted him to their intimacy, and were liberal in promising him " the greatest preferments " should they come
into power.   Before long Swift had another opportunity
which was also a temptation.   The Tory House of Commons had passed the bill against occasional conformity.
Ardent partisans generally approved this bill, as it was
clearly annoying to dissenters.   It was directed against the
practice of qualifying for office by taking the sacrament
according to the rites of the Church of England without
permanently conforming.   It might be fairly argued—
as Defoe argued, though with questionable sincerity—
that such a temporary compliance would be really in

jurious to dissent. The Church would profit by such an
exhibition of the flexibility of its opponents' principles.
Passions were too much heated for such arguments ; and in
the winter of 1703-4, people, says Swift, talked of nothing
else. He was " mightily urged by some great people" to
publish his opinion. An argument from a powerful writer,
and a clergyman, against the bill would be very useful
to his Whig friends. But Swift's high church prejudices
made him hesitate. The Whig leaders assured him that
nothing should induce them to vote against the bill if
they expected its rejection to hurt the church or " do kindness to the dissenters." But it is precarious to argue from
the professed intentions of statesmen to their real motives,
and yet more precarious to argue to the consequences
of their actions. Swift knew not what to think. He
resolved to think no more. At last he made up his mind
to write against the bill, but he made it up too late. The
bill failed to pass ; and Swift felt a relief in dismissing
this delicate subject. He might still call himself a
Whig, and exult in the growth of Whiggism. Meanwhile he persuaded himself that the dissenters and their
troubles were beneath his notice.

They were soon to come again to the front   Swift
came to London at the end of 1707, charged with
a mission on behalf of his church. Queen Anne's
Bounty was founded in 1704. The crown restored
to the church the first-fruits and tenths which Henry
VIII. had diverted from the papal into his own
treasury, and appropriated them to the augmentation of
small livings. It was proposed to get the same boon for
the Church of Ireland. The whole sum amounted to about
1000*l*. a year, with a possibility of an additional 2000*l*.
Swift, who had spoken of this to King, the Archbishop of

Dublin, was now to act as solicitor on behalf of the Irish clergy, and hoped to make use of his influence with Somers and Sunderland. The negotiation was to give him more trouble than he foresaw, and initiate him, before he had done with it, into certain secrets of cabinets and councils which he as yet very imperfectly appreciated. His letters to King, continued over a long period, throw much light on his motives. Swift was in England from November, 1707, till March, 1709. The year 1708 was for him, as he says, a year of suspense, a year of vast importance to his career, and marked by some characteristic utterances. He hoped to use his influence with Somers. Somers, though still out of office, was the great oracle of the Whigs, whilst Sunderland was already Secretary of State. In January, 1708, the bishopric of Waterford was vacant, and Somers tried to obtain the see for Swift. The attempt failed, but the political catastrophe of the next month gave hopes that the influence of Somers would soon be paramount. Harley, the prince of wire-pulling and back-stair intrigue, had exploded the famous Masham plot. Though this project failed, it was "reckoned," says Swift, "the greatest piece of court skill that has been acted many years." Queen Anne was to take advantage of the growing alienation of the church party to break her bondage to the Marlboroughs, and change her ministers. But the attempt was premature, and discomfited its devisers. Harley was turned out of office; Marlborough and Godolphin came into alliance with the Whig junto; and the queen's bondage seemed more complete than ever. A cabinet crisis in those days, however, took a long time. It was not till October, 1708, that the Whigs, backed by a new Parliament and strengthened by the victory of Oudenarde, were in full enjoyment of power. Somers at last became President of

the Council and Wharton Lord Lieutenant of Ireland.
Wharton's appointment was specially significant for Swift.
He was, as even Whigs admitted, a man of infamous character, redeemed only by energy and unflinching fidelity
to his party. He was licentious and a freethinker ; his infidelity showed itself in the grossest outrages against
common decency. If he had any religious principle it
was a preference of Presbyterians, as sharing his antipathy to the church. No man could be more radically
antipathetic to Swift. Meanwhile, the success of the
Whigs meant in the first instance the success of the men
from whom Swift had promises of preferment. He tried
to use his influence as he had proposed. In June he had
an interview about the first-fruits with Godolphin, to
whom he had been recommended by Somers and Sunderland. Godolphin replied in vague officialisms, suggesting
with studied vagueness that the Irish clergy must show
themselves more grateful than the English. His meaning,
as Swift thought, was that the Irish clergy should consent
to a repeal of the Test Act, regarded by them and by him
as the essential bulwark of the Church. Nothing definite,
however, was said ; and meanwhile Swift, though he gave
no signs of compliance, continued to hope for his own preferment. When the final triumph of the Whigs came he
was still hoping, though with obvious qualms as to his
position. He begged King (in Nov. 1708) to believe in
his fidelity to the church. Offers might be made to him, but
"no prospect of making my fortune shall ever prevail on
me to go against what becomes a man of conscience and
truth, and an entire friend to the established church." He
hoped that he might be appointed secretary to a projected
embassy to Vienna, a position which would put him
beyond the region of domestic politics.

Meanwhile he had published certain tracts which may

be taken as the manifesto of his faith at the time when his principles were being most severely tested. Would he or would he not sacrifice his churchmanship to the interests of the party with which he was still allied? There can be no doubt that by an open declaration of Whig principles in church matters—such a declaration, say, as would have satisfied Burnet—he would have qualified himself for preferment, and have been in a position to command the fulfilment of the promises made by Somers and Sunderland.

The writings in question were the *Argument to prove the inconvenience of abolishing Christianity;* a *Project for the Advancement of Religion;* and the *Sentiments of a Church of England Man.* The first, as I have said, was meant to show that the satirical powers which had given offence in the *Tale of a Tub,* could be applied without equivocation in defence of Christianity. The *Project* is a very forcible exposition of a text which is common enough in all ages—namely, that the particular age of the writer is one of unprecedented corruption, It shares, however, with Swift's other writings, the merit of downright sincerity, which convinces us that the author is not repeating platitudes, but giving his own experience and speaking from conviction. His proposals for a reform, though he must have felt them to be chimerical, are conceived in the spirit common in the days before people had begun to talk about the State and the individual. He assumes throughout that a vigorous action of the court and the government will reform the nation. He does not contemplate the now commonplace objection that such a revival of the Puritanical system might simply stimulate hypocrisy. He expressly declares that religion may be brought into fashion " by the power of the administration," and assumes that to bring religion into fashion is

the same thing as to make men religious. This view—
suitable enough to Swift's imperious temper—was also the
general assumption of the time. A suggestion thrown out
in his pamphlet is generally said to have led to the scheme
soon afterwards carried out under Harley's administration
for building fifty new churches in London. A more
personal touch is Swift's complaint that the clergy sacrifice
their influence by "sequestering themselves" too much,
and forming a separate caste. This reads a little like an
implied defence of himself for frequenting London coffee-
houses, when cavillers might have argued that he should
be at Laracor. But like all Swift's utterances, it covered a
settled principle. I have already noticed this peculiarity,
which he shows elsewhere when describing himself as

> A clergyman of special note
> For shunning others of his coat ;
> Which made his brethren of the gown
> Take care betimes to run him down.

The *Sentiments of a Church of England Man* is more significant. It is a summary of his unvarying creed. In politics
he is a good Whig. He interprets the theory of passive obedience as meaning obedience to the " legislative power;" not
therefore to the king specially ; and he deliberately accepts
the revolution on the plain ground of the *salus populi*. His
leading maxim is that the " administration cannot be
placed in too few hands nor the legislature in too many."
But this political liberality is associated with unhesitating
churchmanship. Sects are mischievous : to say that they
are mischievous is to say that they ought to be checked
in their beginning ; where they exist they should be
tolerated, but not to the injury of the church. And
hence he reaches his leading principle that a " govern-

ment cannot give them (sects) too much ease, nor trust
them with too little power." Such doctrines clearly and
tersely laid down were little to the taste of the Whigs,
who were more anxious than ever to conciliate the dissenters. But it was not till the end of the year that
Swift applied his abstract theory to a special case. There
had been various symptoms of a disposition to relax the
Test Acts in Ireland. The appointment of Wharton to be
Lord Lieutenant was enough to alarm Swift, even though
his friend Addison was to be Wharton's secretary. In
December, 1708, he published a pamphlet, ostensibly a letter from a member of the Irish to a member of the English
House of Commons, in which the necessity of keeping up
the Test was vigorously enforced. It is the first of Swift's
political writings in which we see his true power. In those
just noticed he is forced to take an impartial tone. He
is trying to reconcile himself to his alliance with the Whigs,
or to reconcile the Whigs to their protection of himself. He
speaks as a moderator, and poses as the dignified moralist
above all party-feeling. But in this letter he throws the
reins upon his humour, and strikes his opponents full in
the face. From his own point of view the pamphlet is
admirable. He quotes Cowley's verse,

> Forbid it, heaven, my life should be
> Weighed with thy least conveniency.

The Irish, by which he means the English, and the English
exclusively of the Scotch, in Ireland, represent this enthusiastic lover, and are called upon to sacrifice themselves
to the political conveniency of the Whig party. Swift
expresses his usual wrath against the Scots, who are
eating up the land, boasts of the loyalty of the Irish
Church, and taunts the Presbyterians with their tyranny

in former days. Am I to be forced, he asks, "to keep
my chaplain disguised like my butler, and steal to prayers
in a back room, as my grandfather used in those times
when the Church of England was malignant?" Is not
this a ripping up of old quarrels? Ought not all Protestants to unite against Papists? No, the enemy is
the same as ever. "It is agreed among naturalists
that a lion is a larger, a stronger, and more dangerous
enemy than a cat ; yet if a man were to have his choice,
either a lion at his foot fast bound with three or four
chains, his teeth drawn out, and his claws pared to the
quick, or an angry cat in full liberty at his throat, he
would take no long time to determine." The bound lion
means the Catholic natives, whom Swift declares to be as
"inconsiderable as the women and children."

Meanwhile the long first-fruits negotiation was languidly
proceeding. At last it seemed to be achieved. Lord
Pembroke, the outgoing Lord Lieutenant, sent Swift
word that the grant had been made. Swift reported his
success to Archbishop King with a very pardonable touch of
complacency at his "very little" merit in the matter.
But a bitter disappointment followed. The promise made
had never been fulfilled. In March, 1709, Swift had
again to write to the Archbishop, recounting his failure,
his attempt to remonstrate with Wharton, the new Lord
Lieutenant, and the too certain collapse of the whole
business. The failure was complete ; the promised boon
was not granted, and Swift's chance of a bishopric had
pretty well vanished. Halifax, the great Whig Mæcenas,
and the Bufo of Pope, wrote to him in his retirement at
Dublin, declaring that he had "entered into a confederacy
with Mr. Addison" to urge Swift's claims upon Government, and speaking of the declining health of South,

then a Prebendary of Westminster. Swift endorsed this " I lock up this letter as a true original of courtiers and court promises," and wrote in a volume he had begged from the same person that it was the only favour " he ever received from him or his party." In the last months of his stay he had suffered cruelly from his old giddiness, and he went to Ireland, after a visit to his mother in Leicester, in sufficiently gloomy mood; retired to Laracor, and avoided any intercourse with the authorities at the Castle, excepting always Addison.

To this it is necessary to add one remark. Swift's version of the story is substantially that which I have given, and it is everywhere confirmed by contemporary letters. It shows that he separated from the Whig party when at the height of their power, and separated because he thought them opposed to the church principles which he advocated from first to last. It is most unjust, therefore to speak of Swift as a deserter from the Whigs, because he afterwards joined the church party, which shared all his strongest prejudices. I am so far from seeing any ground for such a charge, that I believe that few men have ever adhered more strictly to the principles with which they have started. But such charges have generally an element of truth; and it is easy here to point out what was the really weak point in Swift's position.

Swift's writings, with one or two trifling exceptions, were originally anonymous. As they were very apt to produce warrants for the apprehension of publisher and author, the precaution was natural enough in later years. The mask was often merely ostensible; a sufficient protection against legal prosecution, but in reality covering an open secret. When in the *Sentiments of a Church of England Man* Swift professes to conceal his name care-

fully, it may be doubted how far this is to be taken
seriously.   But he went much further in the letter on the
Test Act.   He inserted a passage intended really to blind
his adversaries by a suggestion that Dr. Swift was likely
to write in favour of abolishing the test ; and he even
complains to King of the unfairness of this treatment.
His assault, therefore, upon the supposed Whig policy
was clandestine.   This may possibly be justified ; he
might even urge that he was still a Whig, and was warning ministers against measures which they had not yet
adopted, and from which, as he thinks, they may still be
deterred by an alteration of the real Irish feeling.[7]   He
complained afterwards that he was ruined—that is, as to
his chances of preferment from the party—by the suspicion
of his authorship of this tract.   That is to say, he was
" ruined " by the discovery of his true sentiments.   This
is to admit that he was still ready to accept preferment
from the men whose supposed policy he was bitterly attacking, and that he resented their alienation as a grievance.
The resentment indeed was most bitter and pertinacious.   He
turned savagely upon his old friends because they would
not make him a bishop.   The answer from their point of
view was conclusive.   He had made a bitter and covert
attack, and he could not at once claim a merit from
churchmen for defending the church against the Whigs,
and revile the Whigs for not rewarding him.   But incon-
sistency of this kind is characteristic of Swift.   He
thought the Whigs scoundrels for not patronizing him,
and not the less scoundrels because their conduct was
consistent with their own scoundrelly principles.   People
who differ from me must be wicked, argued this consistent

---

[7] Letter to King, Jan. 6th, 1709.

egotist, and their refusal to reward me is only an additional
wickedness.   The case appeared to him as though he had
been a Nathan sternly warning a David of his sins, and
for that reason deprived of honour.   David could not have
urged his sinful desires as an excuse for ill-treatment of
Nathan.   And Swift was inclined to class indifference to
the welfare of the church as a sin even in an avowed
Whig.   Yet he had to ordinary minds forfeited any right
to make non-fulfilment a grievance, when he ought to have
regarded performance as a disgrace.

CHAPTER V.

In the autumn of 1710 Swift was approaching the end of his forty-third year. A man may well feel at forty-two that it is high time that a post should have been assigned to him. Should an opportunity be then, and not till then, put in his way, he feels that he is throwing for heavy stakes ;· and that failure, if failure should follow, would be irretrievable. Swift had been longing vainly for an opening. In the remarkable letter (of April, 1722) from which I have quoted the anecdote of the lost fish, he says that, " all my endeavours from a boy to distinguish myself were only for want of a great title and fortune, that I might be used like a lord by those who have an opinion of my parts ; whether right or wrong is no great matter ; and so the reputation of wit or great learning does the office of a blue riband or of a coach and six horses." The phrase betrays Swift's scornful self-mockery; that inverted hypocrisy which led him to call his motives by their worst names, and to disavow what he might have been sorry to see denied by others. But, like all that Swift says of himself, it also expresses a genuine conviction. Swift was ambitious, and his ambition meant an absolute need of imposing his will upon others. He was a man born to rule; not to affect thought, but to control

conduct. He was therefore unable to find full occupation,
though he might seek occasional distraction, in literary
pursuits. Archbishop King, who had a strange knack of
irritating his correspondent—not, it seems, without intention—annoyed Swift intensely in 1711 by advising
him (most superfluously) to get preferment, and with that
view to write a serious treatise upon some theological
question. Swift, who was in the thick of his great
political struggle, answered that it was absurd to ask a
man floating at sea what he meant to do when he got
ashore. "Let him get there first and rest and dry himself, and then look about him." To find firm footing
amidst the welter of political intrigues, was Swift's first
object. Once landed in a deanery he might begin to think
about writing ; but he never attempted, like many men in
his position, to win preferment through literary achievements. To a man of such a temperament, his career must
so far have been cruelly vexatious. We are generally
forced to judge of a man's life by a few leading incidents ;
and we may be disposed to infer too hastily that the
passions roused on those critical occasions coloured the
whole tenor of every-day existence. Doubtless Swift
was not always fretting over fruitless prospects. He was
often eating his dinner in peace and quiet, and even
amusing himself with watching the Moor Park rooks or
the Laracor trout. Yet it is true that so far as a man's
happiness depends upon the consciousness of a satisfactory
employment of his faculties, whether with a view to glory
or solid comfort, Swift had abundant causes of discontent.
The "conjured spirit" was still weaving ropes of sand.
For ten years he had been dependent upon Temple, and
his struggles to get upon his own legs had been fruitless :
on Temple's death he managed when past thirty to wring

from fortune a position of bare independence, not of satisfying activity, he had not gained a fulcrum from which to move the world, but only a bare starting-point whence he might continue to work. The promises from great men had come to nothing. He might perhaps have realized them, could he have consented to be faithless to his dearest convictions ; the consciousness that he had so far sacrificed his position to his principles gave him no comfort, though it nourished his pride. His enforced reticence produced an irritation against the ministers whom it had been intended to conciliate, which deepened into bitter resentment for their neglect. The year and a half passed in Ireland during 1709-10 was a period in which his day-dreams must have had a background of disappointed hopes. "I stayed above half the time," he says, "in one scurvy acre of ground, and I always left it with regret." He shut himself up at Laracor, and nourished a growing indignation against the party represented by Wharton.

Yet events were moving rapidly in England, and opening a new path for his ambition. The Whigs were in full possession of power, though at the price of a growing alienation of all who were weary of a never-ending war, or hostile to the Whig policy in Church and State. The leaders, though warned by Somers, fancied that they would strengthen their position by attacking the defeated enemy. The prosecution of Sacheverell in the winter of 1709-10, if not directed by personal spite, was meant to intimidate the high-flying Tories. It enabled the Whig leaders to indulge in a vast quantity of admirable constitutional rhetoric ; but it supplied the High Church party with a martyr and a cry, and gave the needed impetus to the growing discontent. The queen took heart to revolt

against the Marlboroughs ; the Whig Ministry were turned
out of office ; Harley became Chancellor of the Exchequer
in August ; and the parliament was dissolved in September,
1710, to be replaced in November by one in which the
Tories had an overwhelming majority.

We are left to guess at the feelings with which Swift
contemplated these changes. Their effect upon his personal
prospects was still problematical. In spite of his wrathful
retirement, there was no open breach between him and
the Whigs. He had no personal relations with the new
possessors of power. Harley and St. John, the two chiefs,
were unknown to him. And, according to his own statement, he started for England once more with great
reluctance in order again to take up the weary Firstfruits
negociation. Wharton, whose hostility had intercepted
the proposed bounty, went with his party, and was succeeded by the High Church Duke of Ormond. The
political aspects were propitious for a renewed application,
and Swift's previous employment pointed him out as the
most desirable agent.

And now Swift suddenly comes into full light. For
two or three years we can trace his movements day by
day ; follow the development of his hopes and fears ;
and see him more clearly than he could be seen by
almost any of his contemporaries. The famous *Journal to
Stella*, a series of letters written to Esther Johnson and
Mrs. Dingley, from September, 1710, till April, 1713, is
the main and central source of information. Before telling
the story, a word or two may be said of the nature of
this document, one of the most interesting that ever
threw light upon the history of a man of genius. The
Journal is one of the very few that were clearly written
without the faintest thought of publication. There is no

indication of any such intention in the *Journal to Stella.*
It never occurred to Swift that it could ever be seen by
any but the persons primarily interested.   The journal
rather shuns politics ; they will·not interest his correspondent, and he is afraid of the post-office clerks—then
and long afterwards often employed as spies.   Inter-
views with ministers have scarcely more prominence than
the petty incidents of his daily life.   We are told that he
discussed business, but the discussion is not reported.
Much more is omitted which might have been of the
highest interest.   We hear of meetings with Addison ;
not a phrase of Addison's is vouchsafed to us ; we go to
the door of Harley or St. John ; we get no distinct vision
of the men who were the centres of all observation.   Nor,
again, are there any of those introspective passages which
give to some journals the interest of a confession.   What,
then, is the interest of the *Journal to Stella ?* One
element of strange and singular fascination, to be considered hereafter, is the prattle with his correspondent.
For the rest, our interest depends in great measure upon
the reflections with which we must ourselves clothe the
bare skeleton of facts.   In reading the *Journal to Stella*
we may fancy ourselves waiting in a parliamentary
lobby during an excited debate.   One of the chief actors
hurries out at intervals ; pours out a kind of hasty
bulletin ; tells of some thrilling incident, or indicates
some threatening symptom ; more frequently he seeks to
relieve his anxieties by indulging in a little personal
gossip, and only interjects such comments upon politics as
can be compressed into a hasty ejaculation, often, as may
be supposed, of the imprecatory kind.   Yet he unconsciously betrays his hopes and fears ; he is fresh from the
thick of the fight, and we perceive that his nerves are

G

still quivering, and that his phrases are glowing with the
ardour of the struggle. Hopes and fears are long since
faded, and the struggle itself is now but a war of phantoms. Yet with the help of the *Journal* and contemporary
documents, we can revive for the moment the decaying
images, and cheat ourselves into the momentary per-
suasion that the fate of the world depends upon Harley's
success, as we now hold it to depend upon Mr. Gladstone's.

Swift reached London on September 7th, 1710 ; the
political revolution was in full action, though Parliament
was not yet dissolved. The Whigs were "ravished to
see him;" they clutched at him, he says, like drowning
men at a twig, and the great men made him their
"clumsy apologies." Godolphin was "short, dry and
morose;" Somers tried to make explanations, which
Swift received with studied coldness. The ever-courteous
Halifax gave him dinners ; and asked him to drink to the
resurrection of the Whigs, which Swift refused unless he
would add " to their reformation." Halifax persevered in
his attentions, and was always entreating him to go down
to Hampton Court; "which will cost me a guinea to his
servants, and twelve shillings coach hire, and I will see
him hanged first." Swift, however, retained his old
friendship with the wits of the party ; dined with Addison
at his retreat in Chelsea, and sent a trifle or two to the
Tatler. The elections began in October; Swift had
to drive through a rabble of Westminster electors,
judiciously agreeing with their sentiments to avoid dead
cats and broken glasses ; and though Addison was elected
("I believe," says Swift, " if he had a mind to be chosen
king, he would hardly be refused"), the Tories were
triumphant in every direction. And meanwhile, the Tory
leaders were delightfully civil.

On the 4th of October Swift was introduced to Harley, getting himself described (with undeniable truth) " as a discontented person, who was ill used for not being Whig enough." The poor Whigs lamentably confess, he says, their ill usage of him, " but I mind them not." Their confession came too late. Harley had received him with open arms, and won not only Swift's adhesion, but his warm personal attachment. The fact is indisputable, though rather curious. Harley appears to us as a shifty and feeble politician, an inarticulate orator, wanting in principles and resolution, who made it his avowed and almost only rule of conduct that a politician should live from hand to mouth.[1] Yet his prolonged influence in Parliament seems to indicate some personal attraction, which was perceptible to his contemporaries, though rather puzzling to us. All Swift's panegyrics leave the secret in obscurity. Harley seems indeed to have been eminently respectable and decorously religious, amiable in personal intercourse, and able to say nothing in such a way as to suggest profundity instead of emptiness. His reputation as a party manager was immense ; and is partly justified by his quick recognition of Swift's extraordinary qualifications. He had inferior scribblers in his pay, including, as we remember with regret, the shifty Defoe. But he wanted a man of genuine ability and character. Some months later the ministers told Swift that they had been afraid of none but him ; and resolved to have him.

They got him. Harley had received him " with the greatest kindness and respect imaginable." Three days later (Oct. 7th) the firstfruits business is discussed, and Harley received the proposals as warmly as became a

[1] Swift to King, July 12, 1711.

friend of the Church, besides overwhelming Swift with
civilities.   Swift is to be introduced to St. John ; to dine
with Harley next Tuesday ; and after an interview of
four hours, the minister sets him down at St. James's
Coffee-house in a hackney coach.   " All this is odd and
comical ! " exclaims Swift ; " he knew my Christian name
very well," and, as we hear next day, begged Swift to come
to him often, but not to his levée : " that was not a place
for friends to meet."   On the 10th of October, within a
week from the first introduction, Harley promises to get
the firstfruits business, over which the Whigs had haggled
for years, settled by the following Sunday.   Swift's exul-
tation breaks out.   On the 14th he declares that he stands
ten times better with the new people than ever he did with
the old, and is forty times more caressed.   The triumph
is sharpened by revenge.   Nothing, he says of the sort
was ever compassed so soon ; "and purely done by my
personal credit with Mr. Harley, who is so excessively
obliging, that I know not what to make of it, unless to
show the rascals of the other side that they used a man
unworthily who deserved better."   A passage on Nov. 8th
sums up his sentiments.   " Why," he says in answer to
something from Stella, " should the Whigs think I came
from Ireland to leave them ? Sure my journey was no
secret !   I protest sincerely, I did all I could to hinder it,
as the dean can tell you, though now I do not repent it.
But who the devil cares what they think ? Am I under
obligations in the least to any of them all ? Rot them
for ungrateful dogs ; I will make them repent their usage
before I leave this place."   The thirst for vengeance may
not be edifying ; the political zeal was clearly not of the
purest ; but in truth, Swift's party prejudices and his
personal resentments are fused into indissoluble unity.

Hatred of Whig principles and resentment of Whig "ill-usage" of himself, are one and the same thing. Meanwhile, Swift was able (on Nov. 4) to announce his triumph to the Archbishop. He was greatly annoyed by an incident, of which he must also have seen the humorous side. The Irish bishops had bethought themselves after Swift's departure that he was too much of a Whig to be an effective solicitor. They proposed therefore to take the matter out of his hands and apply to Ormond, the new Lord Lieutenant. Swift replied indignantly ; the thing was done, however, and he took care to let it be known that the whole credit belonged to Harley, and of course, in a subordinate sense, to himself. Official formalities were protracted for months longer, and formed one excuse for Swift's continued absence from Ireland ; but we need not trouble ourselves with the matter further.

Swift's unprecedented leap into favour meant more than a temporary success. The intimacy with Harley and with St. John rapidly developed. Within a few months, Swift had forced his way into the very innermost circle of official authority. A notable quarrel seems to have given the final impulse to his career. In February, 1711, Harley offered him a fifty-pound note. This was virtually to treat him as a hireling instead of an ally. Swift resented the offer as an intolerable affront. He refused to be reconciled without ample apology, and after long entreaties. His pride was not appeased for ten days, when the reconciliation was sealed by an invitation from Harley to a Saturday dinner.[2] On Saturdays, the Lord

[2] These dinners, it may be noticed, seem to have been held on Thursdays when Harley had to attend the court at Windsor. This may lead to some confusion with the Brothers' Club, which met on Thursdays during the parliamentary session.

Keeper (Harcourt) and the Secretary of State (St.
John) dined alone with Harley : " and at last," says
Swift, in reporting the event, " they have consented to
let me among them on that day." He goes next day, and
already chides Lord Rivers for presuming to intrude into
the sacred circle. " They call me nothing but Jonathan,"
he adds ; " and I said I believed they would leave me
Jonathan, as they found me." These dinners were continued, though they became less select. Harley called
Saturday his " whipping-day ;" and Swift was the
heartiest wielder of the lash. From the same February,
Swift began to dine regularly with St. John every
Sunday ; and we may note it as some indication of the
causes of his later preference of Harley, that on one
occasion he has to leave St. John early. The company,
he says, were in constraint, because he would suffer no
man to swear or talk indecently in his presence.

Swift had thus conquered the ministry at a blow.
What services did he render in exchange ? His extraordinary influence seems to have been due in a measure to
sheer force of personal ascendency. No man could come
into contact with Swift without feeling that magnetic
influence. But he was also doing a more tangible service.
In thus admitting Swift to their intimacy, Harley and
St. John were in fact paying homage to the rising power
of the pen. Political writers had hitherto been hirelings,
and often little better than spies. No preceding, and, we
may add, no succeeding writer ever achieved such a position
by such means. The press has become more powerful as a
whole : but no particular representative of the press has
made such a leap into power. Swift came at the time
when the influence of political writing was already great :
and when the personal favour of a prominent minister

could still work miracles. Harley made him a favourite
of the old stamp, to reward his supremacy in the use of
the new weapon.

Swift had begun in October by avenging himself upon
Godolphin's coldness, in a copy of Hudibrastic verses
about the virtues of Sid Hamet the Magician's Rod—
that is, the treasurer's staff of office—which had a wonderful success. He fell savagely upon the hated Wharton
not long after, in what he calls " a damned libellous
pamphlet," of which 2000 copies were sold in two days.
Libellous, indeed, is a faint epithet to describe a production which, if its statements be true, proves that
Wharton deserved to be hunted from society. Charges
of lying, treachery, atheism, Presbyterianism, debauchery,
indecency, shameless indifference to his own reputation
and his wife's, the vilest corruption and tyranny in his
government are piled upon his victim as thickly as they
will stand. Swift does not expect to sting Wharton.
" I neither love nor hate him," he says. " If I see him
after this is published, he will tell me ' that he is
damnably mauled ;' and then, with the easiest transition
in the world, ask about the weather, or the time of day."
Wharton might possibly think that abuse of this kind
might almost defeat itself by its own virulence. But
Swift had already begun writings of a more statesmanlike
and effective kind.

A paper war was already raging when Swift came to
London. The *Examiner* had been started by St. John,
with the help of Atterbury, Prior, and others ; and,
opposed for a short time by Addison, in the *Whig
Examiner*. Harley, after granting the first-fruits, had told
Swift, that the great want of the ministry was " some
good pen," to keep up the spirits of the party. The

Examiner, however, was in need of a firmer and more
regular manager ; and Swift took it in hand, his first
weekly article appearing November 2nd, 1710, his last on
June 14th, 1711.   His *Examiners* achieved an immediate
and unprecedented success.   And yet to say the truth, a
modern reader is apt to find them decidedly heavy.   No
one, indeed, can fail to perceive the masculine sense, the
terseness and precision of the utterance.   And yet many
writings which produced less effect are far more readable
now.   The explanation is simple, and applies to most of
Swift's political writings.   They are all rather acts than
words.   They are blows struck in a party-contest : and
their merit is to be gauged by their effect.   Swift cares
nothing for eloquence, or logic, or invective—and little, it
must be added, for veracity—so long as he hits his mark.
To judge him by a merely literary standard, is to judge a
fencer by the grace of his attitudes.   Some high literary
merits are implied in efficiency, as real grace is necessary
to efficient fencing : but in either case, a clumsy blow
which reaches the heart is better than the most dexterous
flourish in the air.   Swift's eye is always on the end, as a
good marksman looks at nothing but the target.

   What, then, is Swift's aim in the *Examiner* ?   Mr.
Kinglake has told us how a great journal throve by
discovering what was the remark that was on every one's
lips, and making the remark its own.   Swift had the
more dignified task of really striking the keynote for his
party.   He was to put the ministerial theory into that
form in which it might seem to be the inevitable utterance
of strong common-sense.   Harley's supporters were to see
in Swift's phrases just what they would themselves have
said—if they had been able.   The shrewd, sturdy, narrow
prejudices of the average Englishman were to be pressed

into the service of the ministry, by showing how admirably
they could be clothed in the ministerial formulas.

The real question, again, as Swift saw, was the question
of peace.   Whig and Tory, as he said afterwards,[3] were
really obsolete words.   The true point at issue was peace
or war.   The purpose, therefore, was to take up his ground
so that peace might be represented as the natural policy of
the church or Tory party; and war as the natural fruit
of the selfish Whigs.   It was necessary, at the same time,
to show that this was not the utterance of high-flying
Toryism or downright Jacobitism, but the plain dictate of
a cool and impartial judgment.   He was not to prove but
to take for granted that the war had become intolerably
burdensome; and to express the growing wish for peace
in terms likely to conciliate the greatest number of supporters.   He was to lay down the platform which could
attract as many as possible, both of the zealous Tories and
of the lukewarm Whigs.

Measured by their fitness for this end, the *Examiners*
are admirable.   Their very fitness for the end implies the
absence of some qualities which would have been more
attractive to posterity.   Stirring appeals to patriotic sentiment may suit a Chatham rousing a nation to action;
but Swift's aim is to check the extravagance in the name
of selfish prosaic prudence.   The philosophic reflections of
Burke, had Swift been capable of such reflection, would
have flown above the heads of his hearers.   Even the
polished and elaborate invective of Junius would have
been out of place.   No man, indeed, was a greater master
of invective than Swift.   He shows it in the *Examiners*
by onslaughts upon the detested Wharton.   He shows,

---

[3] *Letter to a Whig Lord,* 1712.

too, that he is not restrained by any scruples when it comes
in his way to attack his old patrons, and he adopts the
current imputations upon their private character.   He
could roundly accuse Cowper of bigamy, and Somers—
the Somers whom he had elaborately praised some years
before in the dedication to the *Tale of a Tub*—of the most
abominable perversion of justice.   But these are taunts
thrown out by the way.   The substance of the articles is
not invective, but profession of political faith.   One great
name, indeed, is of necessity assailed.   Marlborough's
fame was a tower of strength for the Whigs.   His duchess
and his colleagues had fallen ; but whilst war was still
raging, it seemed impossible to dismiss the greatest living
commander.   Yet whilst Marlborough was still in power,
his influence might be used to bring back his party.
Swift's treatment of this great adversary is significant.   He
constantly took credit for having suppressed many attacks [4]
upon Marlborough.   He was convinced that it would be
dangerous for the country to dismiss a general whose very
name carried victory.[5]   He felt that it was dangerous for
the party to make an unreserved attack upon the popular
hero.   Lord Rivers, he says, cursed the *Examiner* to him
for speaking civilly of Marlborough ; and St. John, upon
hearing of this, replied that if the counsels of such men
as Rivers were taken, the ministry "would be blown up
in twenty-four hours."   Yet Marlborough was the war
personified ; and the way to victory lay over Marlborough's
body.   Nor had Swift any regard for the man himself,
who, he says,[6] is certainly a vile man, and has no sort of
merit except the military—as " covetous as hell, and as

[4] *Journal to Stella*, Feb. 6th, 1712, and Jan. 8th and 25th,
1712.
[5] *Ib*. Jan. 7th, 1711.   [6] *Ib*. Jan. 21st, 1712.

ambitious as the prince of it." [7]   The whole case of the
ministry implied the condemnation of Marlborough. Most
modern historians would admit that continuance of the war
could at this time be desired only by fanatics or interested
persons. A psychologist might amuse himself by inquiring what were the actual motives of its advocates ; in
what degrees personal ambition, a misguided patriotism,
or some more sordid passions were blended. But in the
ordinary dialect of political warfare there is no room
for such refinements. The theory of Swift and Swift's
patrons was simple. The war was the creation of the
Whig "ring ;" it was carried on for their own purposes
by the stock-jobbers and "monied men," whose rise was a
new political phenomenon, and who had introduced the
diabolical contrivance of public debts. The landed interest
and the church had been hoodwinked too long by the
union of corrupt interests supported by Dutchmen,
Scotchmen, dissenters, freethinkers, and other manifestations of the evil principle. Marlborough was the head and
patron of the whole. And what was Marlborough's
motive ? The answer was simple. It was that which
has been assigned, with even more emphasis, by Macaulay
—Avarice. The twenty-seventh *Examiner* (Feb. 8th,
1711) probably contains the compliments to which Rivers
objected. Swift, in fact, admits that Marlborough had
all the great qualities generally attributed to him ; but all
are spoilt by this fatal blemish. How far the accusation
was true matters little. It is put at least with force and
dignity ; and it expressed in the pithiest shape Swift's
genuine conviction, that the war now meant corrupt self-
interest. Invective, as Swift knew well enough in his

[7] *Ib.* Dec. 31st, 1710.

cooler moments, is a dangerous weapon, apt to recoil on
the assailant unless it carries conviction.   The attack on
Marlborough does not betray personal animosity; but
the deliberate and the highly plausible judgment of a man
determined to call things by their right names, and not to
be blinded by military glory.

This, indeed, is one of the points upon which Swift's
Toryism was unlike that of some later periods. He always
disliked and despised soldiers and their trade.   " It will
no doubt be a mighty comfort to our grandchildren," he
says in another pamphlet,[8] " when they see a few rags hung
up in Westminster Hall which cost a hundred millions,
whereof they are paying the arrears, to boast as beggars do
that their grandfathers were rich and great."   And in
other respects he has some right to claim the adhesion of
thorough Whigs.   His personal attacks, indeed, upon the
party have a questionable sound.   In his zeal he constantly
forgets that the corrupt ring which he denounces were the
very men from whom he expected preferment.   " I well
remember," he says[9] elsewhere, " the clamours often raised
during the late reign of that party (the Whigs) against
the leaders by those who thought their merits were
not rewarded; and they had, no doubt, reason on their
side, because it is, no doubt, a misfortune to forfeit
honour and conscience for nothing "—rather an awkward
remark from a man who was calling Somers " a false,
deceitful rascal " for not giving him a bishopric ! His
eager desire to make the "ungrateful dogs" repent their
ill-usage of him prompts attacks which injure his own
character with that of his former associates.   But he has
some ground for saying that Whigs have changed their

   [8] *Conduct of the Allies.*   [9] *Advice to October Club.*

principles, in the sense that their dislike of prerogative
and of standing armies had curiously declined when the
Crown and the army came to be on their side.   Their
enjoyment of power had made them soften some of
the prejudices learnt in days of depression.   Swift's dislike of what we now call "militarism" really went deeper
than any party sentiment; and in that sense, as we shall
hereafter see, it had really most affinity with a radicalism
which would have shocked Whigs and Tories alike.   But
in this particular case it fell in with the Tory sentiment.
The masculine vigour of the *Examiners* served the ministry,
who were scarcely less in danger from the excessive zeal
of their more bigoted followers than from the resistance
of the Whig minority.   The pig-headed country squires
had formed an October Club, to muddle themselves with
beer and politics, and hoped—good honest souls—to drive
ministers into a genuine attack on the corrupt practices
of their predecessors.   All Harley's skill in intriguing and
wire-pulling would be needed.   The ministry, said Swift
(on March 4th), "stood like an isthmus" between Whigs
and violent Tories.   He trembled for the result.   They are
able seamen, but the tempest "is too great, the ship too
rotten, and the crew all against them."   Somers had been
twice in the queen's closet.   The Duchess of Somerset,
who had succeeded the Duchess of Marlborough, might be
trying to play Mrs. Masham's game.   Harley, "though
the most fearless man alive," seemed to be nervous, and
was far from well.   "Pray God preserve his health,"
says Swift; "everything depends upon it."   Four days
later, Swift is in an agony.   "My heart," he exclaims,
"is almost broken."   Harley had been stabbed by Guis-
card (March 8th, 1711) at the council-board.   Swift's
letters and journals show an agitation, in which personal

affection seems to be even stronger than political anxiety. "Pray pardon my distraction," he says to Stella, in broken sentences. "I now think of all his kindness to me. The poor creature now lies stabbed in his bed by a desperate French popish villain. Good night, and God bless you both, and pity me; I want it." He wrote to King under the same excitement. Harley, he says, "has always treated me with the tenderness of a parent, and never refused me any favour I asked for a friend; therefore I hope your Grace will excuse the character of this letter." He apologizes again in a postscript for his confusion; it must be imputed to the "violent pain of mind I am in —greater than ever I felt in my life." The danger was not over for three weeks. The chief effect seems to have been that Harley became popular as the intended victim of an hypothetical Popish conspiracy; he introduced an applauded financial scheme in Parliament after his recovery, and was soon afterwards made Earl of Oxford by way of consolation. "This man," exclaimed Swift, "has grown by persecutions, turnings out, and stabbings. What waiting and crowding and bowing there will be at his levee!"

Swift had meanwhile (April 26) retired to Chelsea "for the air," and to have the advantage of a compulsory walk into town (two miles, or 5748 steps each way, he calculates). He was liable, indeed, to disappointment on a rainy day, when "all the three stage-coaches" were taken up by the "cunning natives of Chelsea;" but he got a lift to town in a gentleman's coach for a shilling. He bathed in the river on the hot nights, with his Irish servant, Patrick, standing on the bank to warn off passing boats. The said Patrick, who is always getting drunk, whom Swift cannot find it in his heart to dismiss in England, who

atones for his general carelessness and lying by buying a
linnet for Dingley, making it wilder than ever in his
attempts to tame it, is a characteristic figure in the journal.
In June Swift gets ten days' holiday at Wycombe, and in
the summer he goes down pretty often with the ministers
to Windsor. He came to town in two hours and forty
minutes on one occasion : " twenty miles are nothing
here."   The journeys are described in one of the happiest
of his occasional poems—

> " 'Tis (let me see) three years or more
> (October next it will be four)
> Since Harley bid me first attend
> And chose me for an humble friend :
> Would take me in his coach to chat
> And question me of this or that :
> As " What's o'clock ? " and " How's the wind ? "
> " Whose chariot's that we left behind ? "
> Or gravely try to read the lines
> Writ underneath the country signs.
> Or, " Have you nothing new to-day,
> From Pope, from Parnell, or from Gay ? "
> Such tattle often entertains
> My lord and me as far as Staines,
> As once a week we travel down
> To Windsor, and again to town,
> Where all that passes *inter nos*
> Might be proclaimed at Charing Cross.

And when, it is said, St. John was disgusted by the
frivolous amusements of his companions ; and his political
discourses might be interrupted by Harley's exclamation,
" Swift, I am up ; there's a cat "—the first who saw a cat
or an old woman, winning the game.

Swift and Harley were soon playing a more exciting
game. Prior had been sent to France to renew peace
negotiations, with eladorate mystery. Even Swift was

kept in ignorance.   On his return Prior was arrested by
officious custom-house officers, and the fact of his journey
became public.   Swift took advantage of the general
interest by a pamphlet intended to " bite the town."   Its
political purpose, according to Swift, was to " furnish fools
with something to talk of ;" to draw a false scent across
the trail of the angry and suspicious Whigs.   It seems
difficult to believe that any such effect could be produced
or anticipated ; but the pamphlet, which purports to be
an account of Prior's journey given by a French valet,
desirous of passing himself off as a secretary, is an amusing
example of Swift's power of grave simulation of realities.
The peace negotiations brought on a decisive political
struggle.   Parliament was to meet in September.   The
Whigs resolved to make a desperate effort.   They had
lost the House of Commons, but were still strong in the
Peers.   The Lords were not affected by the rapid oscilla-
tions of public opinion.   They were free from some of
the narrower prejudices of country squires, and true to a
revolution which gave the chief power for more than a
century to the aristocracy : while the recent creations had
ennobled the great Whig leaders, and filled the bench with
low churchmen.   Marlborough and Godolphin had come
over to the Whig junto, and an additional alliance was
now made.   Nottingham had been passed over by Harley,
as it seems, for his extreme Tory principles.   In his
wrath, he made an agreement with the other extreme.   By
one of the most disgraceful bargains of party history,
Nottingham was to join the Whigs in attacking the peace,
whilst the Whigs were to buy his support by accepting
the Occasional Conformity Bill—the favourite high church
measure.   A majority in the House of Lords could not
indeed determine the victory.   The Government of Eng-

land, says Swift in 1715,[1] "cannot move a step while the House of Commons continues to dislike proceedings or persons employed." But the plot went further. The House of Lords might bring about a deadlock, as it had done before. The queen, having thrown off the rule of the Duchess of Marlborough, had sought safety in the rule of two mistresses, Mrs. Masham and the Duchess of Somerset. The Duchess of Somerset was in the Whig interest; and her influence with the queen caused the gravest anxiety to Swift and the ministry. She might induce Anne to call back the Whigs, and in a new House of Commons, elected under a Whig ministry wielding the crown influence and appealing to the dread of a discreditable peace, the majority might be reversed. Meanwhile Prince Eugene was expected to pay a visit to England, bringing fresh proposals for war, and stimulating by his presence the enthusiasm of the Whigs.

Towards the end of September the Whigs began to pour in a heavy fire of pamphlets, and Swift rather meanly begs the help of St. John and the law. But he is confident of victory. Peace is certain; and a peace "very much to the honour and advantage of England." The Whigs are furious; "but we'll wherret them, I warrant, boys." Yet he has misgivings. The news comes of the failure of the Tory expedition against Quebec, which was to have anticipated the policy and the triumphs of Chatham. Harley only laughs as usual; but St. John is cruelly vexed, and begins to suspect his colleagues of suspecting him. Swift listens to both, and tries to smooth matters; but he is growing serious. "I am half weary of them all," he exclaims, and begins to talk of

[1] *Behaviour of Queen's Ministry.*

H

retiring to Ireland.   Harley has a slight illness, and Swift
is at once in a fright. "We are all undone without him,"
he says, "so pray for him, sirrahs ! "   Meanwhile, as the
parliamentary struggle comes nearer, Swift launches the
pamphlet which has been his summer's work.   The
Conduct of the Allies is intended to prove what he had
taken for granted in the *Examiners*.   It is to show, that
is, that the war has ceased to be demanded by national
interests.   We ought always to have been auxiliaries ; we
chose to become principals ; and have yet so conducted the
war that all the advantages have gone to the Dutch.   The
explanation of course is the selfishness or corruption of
the great Whig junto.   The pamphlet, forcible and terse
in the highest degree, had a success due in part to other
circumstances.   It was as much a State paper as a
pamphlet ; a manifesto obviously inspired by the ministry
and containing the facts and papers which were to serve
in the coming debates.   It was published on Nov. 27th ;
on December 1st the second edition was sold in five hours ;
and by the end of January 11,000 copies had been sold.
The parliamentary struggle began on December 7th ; and
the amendment to the address, declaring that no peace
could be safe which left Spain to the Bourbons, was
moved by Nottingham, and carried by a small majority.
Swift had foreseen this danger ; he had begged ministers
to work up the majority ; and the defeat was due to
Harley's carelessness.   It was Swift's temper to anticipate
though not to yield to the worst.   He could see nothing
but ruin.   Every rumour increased his fears,   The queen
had taken the hand of the Duke of Somerset on leaving
the House of Lords, and refused Shrewsbury's.   She must
be going over.   Swift, in his despair, asked St. John to
find him some foreign post, where he might be out of

harm's way if the Whigs should triumph. St. John
laughed and affected courage, but Swift refused to be
comforted. Harley told him that " all would be well ;"
but Harley for the moment had lost his confidence. A
week after the vote he looks upon the ministry as certainly
ruined ; and " God knows," he adds, " what may be the
consequences." By degrees a little hope began to appear ;
though the ministry, as Swift still held, could expect
nothing till the Duchess of Somerset was turned out. By
way of accelerating this event, he hit upon a plan, which
he had reason to repent, and which nothing but his excitement could explain. He composed and printed one of
his favourite squibs, the *Windsor Prophecy*, and though
Mrs. Masham persuaded him not to publish it, distributed
too many copies for secrecy to be possible. In this production, now dull enough, he calls the duchess " carrots,"
as a delicate hint at her red hair, and says that she murdered her second husband.[2] These statements, even if
true, were not conciliatory ; and it was folly to irritate without injuring. Meanwhile reports of ministerial plans gave
him a little courage ; and in a day or two the secret was
out. He was on his way to the post on Saturday,
December 28th, when the great news came. The ministry
had resolved on something like a *coup d'état*, to be long
mentioned with horror by all orthodox Whigs and Tories.
" I have broke open my letter," scribbled Swift in a coffee-
house, " and tore it into the bargain, to let you know that

[2] There was enough plausibility in this scandal to give it a
sting. The duchess had left her second husband, a Mr.
Thynne, immediately after the marriage ceremony, and fled to
Holland. There Count Coningsmark paid her his addresses, and,
coming to England, had Mr. Thynne shot by ruffians in Pall Mall.
See the curious case in the *State Trials*, vol. ix.

we are all safe. The queen has made no less than twelve
new peers . . . . and has turned out the Duke of Somerset.
She is awaked at last, and so is Lord Treasurer. I want
nothing now but to see the duchess out. But we shall do
without her. We are all extremely happy. Give me
joy, sirrahs!" The Duke of Somerset was not out;
but a greater event happened within three days; the
Duke of Marlborough was removed from all his employ-
ments. The Tory victory was for the time complete.

Here, too, was the culminating point of Swift's career.
Fifteen months of energetic effort had been crowned with
success. He was the intimate of the greatest men in the
country; and the most powerful exponent of their policy.
No man in England, outside the ministry, enjoyed a
wider reputation. The ball was at his feet; and no
position open to a clergyman beyond his hopes. Yet
from this period begins a decline. He continued to
write, publishing numerous squibs, of which many have
been lost, and occasionally firing a gun of heavier metal.
But nothing came from him having the authoritative and
masterly tone of the *Conduct of the Allies.* His health
broke down. At the beginning of April, 1712, he was
attacked by a distressing complaint; and his old enemy,
giddiness, gave him frequent alarms. The daily journal
ceased, and was not fairly resumed till December, though
its place is partly supplied by occasional letters. The
political contest had changed its character. The centre
of interest was transferred to Utrecht, where negotiations
began in January, to be protracted over fifteen months:
the ministry had to satisfy the demand for peace, without
shocking the national self-esteem. Meanwhile jealousies
were rapidly developing themselves, which Swift watched
with ever-growing anxiety.

Swift's personal influence remained or increased. He
drew closer to Oxford, but was still friendly with St.
John ; and to the public his position seemed more imposing than ever. Swift was not the man to bear his
honours meekly. In the early period of his acquaintance
with St. John (February 12, 1711), he sends the Prime
Minister into the House of Commons, to tell the Secretary
of State that " I would not dine with him if he dined
late." He is still a novice at the Saturday dinners when
the Duke of Shrewsbury appears : Swift whispers that he
does not like to see a stranger among them ; and St.
John has to explain that the Duke has written for leave.
St. John then tells Swift that the Duke of Buckingham
desires his acquaintance. The Duke, replied Swift,
has not made sufficient advances : and he always expects
greater advances from men in proportion to their rank.
Dukes and great men yielded, if only to humour the
pride of this audacious parson : and Swift soon came to
be pestered by innumerable applicants, attracted by his
ostentation of influence. Even ministers applied through
him. " There is not one of them," he says, in January,
1713, " but what will employ me as gravely to speak for
them to Lord Treasurer, as if I were their brother or his."
He is proud of the burden of influence with the great,
though he affects to complain. The most vivid picture of
Swift in all his glory, is in a familiar passage from Bishop
Kennett's diary : —

"Swift," says Kennett, in 1713, "came into the coffee-house,
and had a bow from everybody but me. When I came to the
antechamber to wait before prayers, Dr. Swift was the principal
man of talk and business, and acted as minister of requests.
He was soliciting the Earl of Arran to speak to his brother
the Duke of Ormond to get a chaplain's place established in

the garrison of Hull, for Mr. Fiddes, a clergyman in that neighbourhood, who had lately been in jail, and published sermons to pay fees. He was promising Mr. Thorold to under-take with my Lord Treasurer that according to his petition he should obtain a salary of 200*l.* per annum, as minister of the English Church at Rotterdam. He stopped F. Gwynne, Esq., going in with the red bag to the queen, and told him aloud he had something to say to him from my Lord Treasurer. He talked with the son of Dr. Davenant to be sent abroad, and took out his pocket-book and wrote down several things as *memoranda,* to do for him. He turned to the fire, and took out his gold watch, and telling him the time of day, complained it was very late. A gentleman said, " it was too fast." " How can I help it," says the Doctor, " if the courtiers give me a watch that won't go right? " Then he instructed a young nobleman that the best poet in England was Mr. Pope (a Papist), who had begun a translation of Homer into English verse, for which, he said, he must have them all subscribe. ' For,' says he, ' the author *shall not* begin to print till *I have* a thousand guineas for him.' Lord Treasurer, after leaving the Queen, came through the room, beckoning Dr. Swift to follow him ; both went off just before prayers.

There is undoubtedly something offensive in this blustering self-assertion. "No man," says Johnson, with his usual force, " can pay a more servile tribute to the great than by suffering his liberty in their presence to aggrandize him in his own esteem." Delicacy was not Swift's strong point; his compliments are as clumsy as his invectives are forcible ; and he shows a certain taint of vulgarity in his intercourse with social dignitaries. He is perhaps avenging himself for the humiliations received at Moor Park. He has a Napoleonic absence of magnanimity. He likes to relish his triumph ; to accept the pettiest as well as the greatest rewards ; to flaunt his

splendours in the eyes of the servile as well as to enjoy
the consciousness of real power.   But it would be a great
mistake to infer that this ostentatiousness of authority con-
cealed real servility.   Swift preferred to take the bull by
the horns.   He forced himself upon ministers by self-
assertion ; and he held them in awe of him as the lion-
tamer keeps down the latent ferocity of the wild beast.
He never takes his eye off his subjects, nor lowers his
imperious demeanour.   He retained his influence, as
Johnson observes, long after his services had ceased to be
useful.   And all this demonstrative patronage meant real
and energetic work.   We may note, for example, and it
incidentally confirms Kennett's accuracy, that he was
really serviceable to Davenant,[3] and that Fiddes got the
chaplaincy at Hull.   No man ever threw himself with
more energy into the service of his friends.   He declared
afterwards that in the days of his credit he had done fifty
times more for fifty people, from whom he had received
no obligations, than Temple had done for him.[4]   The
journal abounds in proofs that this was not overstated.
There is " Mr. Harrison," for example, who has written
" some mighty pretty things."   Swift takes him up ;
rescues him from the fine friends who are carelessly
tempting him to extravagance ; tries to start him in a
continuation of the *Tatler ;* exults in getting him a
secretaryship abroad, which he declares to be " the prettiest
post in Europe for a young gentleman ; " and is most
unaffectedly and deeply grieved when the poor lad dies of
a fever.   He is carrying 100*l.* to his young friend, when
he hears of his death.   " I told Parnell I was afraid to
knock at the door, my mind misgave me," he says.   On

[3] Letters from Smalridge and Dr. Davenant in 1713.
[4] Letter to Lord Palmerston, Jan. 29th, 1726.

his way to bring help to Harrison, he goes to see a "poor
poet, one Mr. Diaper, in a nasty garret, very sick," and
consoles him with twenty guineas from Lord Bolingbroke.
A few days before he has managed to introduce Parnell
to Harley, or rather to contrive it so that "the ministry
desire to be acquainted with Parnell, and not Parnell with
the ministry." His old schoolfellow Congreve was in
alarm about his appointments. Swift spoke at once to
Harley, and went off immediately to report his success to
Congreve : "so," he says, "I have made a worthy man
easy, and that is a good day's work."[5] One of the latest
letters in his journal refers to his attempt to serve his
other schoolfellow, Berkeley. "I will favour him as
much as I can," he says ; "this I think I am bound to in
honour and conscience, to use all my little credit toward
helping forward men of worth in the world." He was
always helping less conspicuous men ; and he prided
himself, with justice, that he had been as helpful to
Whigs as to Tories. The ministry complained that he
never came to them "without a Whig in his sleeve."
Besides his friend Congreve, he recommended Rowe for
preferment, and did his best to protect Steele and Addison.
No man of letters ever laboured more heartily to promote
the interests of his fellow-craftsmen, as few have ever had
similar opportunities.

Swift, it is plain, desired to use his influence magnifi-
cently. He hoped to make his reign memorable by
splendid patronage of literature. The great organ of
munificence was the famous Brothers' Club, of which
he was the animating spirit. It was founded in June,
1711, during Swift's absence at Wycombe ; it was intended
to "advance conversation and friendship," and obtain

[5] June 22nd, 1711.

patronage for deserving persons. It was to include none but wits and men able to help wits, and, "if we go on as we begun," says Swift, "no other club in this town will be worth talking of." In March, 1712, it consisted, as Swift tells us, of nine lords and ten commoners.[6] It excluded Harley and the Lord Keeper (Harcourt) apparently as they were to be the distributors of the patronage; but it included St. John and several leading ministers, Harley's son and son-in-law, and Harcourt's son; whilst literature was represented by Swift, Arbuthnot, Prior, and Friend, all of whom were more or less actively employed by the ministry. The club was therefore composed of the ministry and their dependents, though it had not avowedly a political colouring. It dined on Thursday during the Parliamentary session, when the political squibs of the day were often laid on the table, including Swift's famous *Windsor Prophecy*, and subscriptions were sometimes collected for such men as Diaper and Harrison. It flourished, however, for little more than the first season. In the winter of 1712-13 it began to suffer from the common disease of such institutions. Swift began to complain bitterly of the extravagance of the charges. He gets the club to leave a tavern in which the bill[7] "for four dishes and four, first

[6] The list, so far as I can make it out from references in the journal, appears to include more names. One or two had probably retired. The peers are as follows :—The Dukes of Shrewsbury (perhaps only suggested), Ormond and Beaufort; Lords Orrery, Rivers, Dartmouth, Dupplin, Masham, Bathurst, and Lansdowne (the last three were of the famous twelve) ; and the commoners are Swift, Sir R. Raymond, Jack Hill, Disney, Sir W. Wyndham, St. John, Prior, Friend, Arbuthnot, Harley (son of Lord Oxford), and Harcourt (son of Lord Harcourt).

[7] Feb. 28th, 1712.

and second course, without wine and drink," had been
21*l*. 6*s*. 8*d*. The number of guests, it seems, was fourteen.
Next winter the charges are divided. "It cost me nineteen shillings to-day for my club dinner," notes Swift,
Dec. 18, 1712. "I don't like it." Swift had a high
value for every one of the nineteen shillings. The
meetings became irregular: Harley was ready to give
promises, but no patronage: and Swift's attendance falls
off. Indeed, it may be noted that he found dinners and
suppers full of danger to his health. He constantly
complains of their after-effects; and partly perhaps for that
reason he early ceases to frequent coffee-houses. Perhaps
too his contempt for coffee-house society, and the increasing
dignity which made it desirable to keep possible applicants
at a distance, had much to do with this. The Brothers'
Club, however, was long remembered by its members, and
in later years they often address each other by the old
fraternal title.

One design which was to have signalized Swift's period
of power, suggested the only paper which he had ever published with his name. It was a "proposal for correcting, im-
proving, and ascertaining the English language," published
in May, 1712, in the form of a letter to Harley. The
letter itself, written offhand in six hours (Feb. 21, 1712),
is not of much value; but Swift recurs to the subject
frequently enough to show that he really hoped to be the
founder of an English Academy. Had Swift been his
own minister instead of the driver of a minister, the
project might have been started. The rapid development
of the political struggle sent Swift's academy to the limbo
provided for such things; and few English authors will
regret the failure of a scheme unsuited to our natural

idiosyncrasy, and calculated, as I fancy, to end in nothing
but an organization of pedantry.

One remark meanwhile occurs which certainly struck
Swift himself.   He says (March 17, 1712) that Sacheverel,
the Tory martyr, has come to him for patronage, and
observes that when he left Ireland neither of them could
have anticipated such a relationship.   " This," he adds,
" is the seventh I have now provided for since I came,
and can do nothing for myself."   Hints at a desire for
preferment do not appear for some time ; but as he is constantly speaking of an early return to Ireland, and is as
regularly held back by the entreaties of the ministry, there
must have been at least an implied promise.   A hint had
been given that he might be made chaplain to Harley, when
the minister became Earl of Oxford.   " I will be no man's
chaplain alive," he says.   He remarks about the same time
(May 23, 1711) that it " would look extremely little " if
he returned without some distinction ; but he will not
beg for preferment.   The ministry, he says in the following
August, only want him for one bit of business (the *Conduct of the Allies* presumably).   When that is done, he
will take his leave of them.   " I never got a penny from
them nor expect it."   The only post for which he made
a direct application was that of historiographer.   He had
made considerable preparations for his so-called *History of
the Last Four Years of Queen Anne*, which appeared
posthumously ; and which may be described as one of his
political pamphlets without the vigour[8]—a dull statement

[8] Its authenticity was doubted, but, as I think, quite gratuitously, by Johnson, by Lord Stanhope, and, as Stanhope says, by
Macaulay.   The dulness is easily explicable by the circumstances
of the composition.

of facts put together by a partisan affecting the historical
character. This application, however, was not made till
April, 1714, when Swift was possessed of all the preferment that he was destined to receive. He considered in
his haughty way that he should be entreated rather than
entreat; and ministers were perhaps slow to give him anything which could take him away from them. A secret
influence was at work against him. The *Tale of a Tub*
was brought up against him; and imputations upon his
orthodoxy were common. Nottingham even revenged
himself by describing Swift in the House of Lords as a
divine " who is hardly suspected of being a Christian."
Such insinuations were also turned to account by the
Duchess of Somerset, who retained her influence over
Anne in spite of Swift's attacks. His journal in the
winter of 1712-13 shows growing discontent. In December, 1712, he resolves to write no more till something is
done for him. He will get under shelter before he makes
more enemies. He declares that he is " soliciting nothing "
(February 4, 1713), but he is growing impatient. Harley
is kinder than ever. " Mighty kind! " exclaims Swift,
" with a ——; less of civility and more of interest;" or
as he puts it in one of his favourite " proverbs " soon
afterwards—" my grandmother used to say,—

> More of your lining
> And less of your dining."

At last Swift, hearing that he was again to be passed over,
gave a positive intimation that he would retire if nothing
was done; adding that he should complain of Harley for
nothing but neglecting to inform him sooner of the hopelessness of his position.[9] The dean of St. Patrick's was at

[9] April 13, 1713.

last promoted to a bishopric, and Swift appointed to the vacant deanery. The warrant was signed on April 23, and in June Swift set out to take possession of his deanery. It was no great prize; he would have to pay 1000*l.* for the house and fees, and thus, he says, it would be three years before he would be the richer for it; and, moreover, it involved what he already described as "banishment" to a country which he hated.

His state of mind when entering upon his preferment was painfully depressed. "At my first coming," he writes to Miss Vanhomrigh, "I thought I should have died with discontent; and was horribly melancholy while they were installing me; but it begins to wear off, and change to dulness." This depression is singular, when we remember that Swift was returning to the woman for whom he had the strongest affection, and from whom he had been separated for nearly three years; and moreover, that he was returning as a famous and a successful man. He seems to have been received with some disfavour by a society of Whig proclivities; he was suffering from a fresh return of ill-health; and besides the absence from the political struggles in which he was so keenly interested, he could not think of them without deep anxiety. He returned to London in October at the earnest request of political friends. Matters were looking serious; and though the journal to Stella was not again taken up, we can pretty well trace the events of the following period.

There can rarely have been a less congenial pair of colleagues than Harley and St. John. Their union was that of a still more brilliant, daring, and self-confident Disraeli with a very inferior edition of Sir Robert Peel, with smaller intellect and exaggerated infirmities. The timidity, procrastination, and "refinement" of the Trea-

surer were calculated to exasperate his audacious colleague.
From the earliest period Swift had declared that everything depended upon the good mutual understanding of
the two; he was frightened by every symptom of discord,
and declares (in August, 1711) that he has ventured all his
credit with the Ministers to remove their differences. He
knew, as he afterwards said (October 20, 1711), that this
was the way to be sent back to his willows at Laracor,
but everything must be risked in such a case. When
difficulties revived next year he hoped that he had made
a reconciliation. But the discord was too vital. The
victory of the Tories brought on a serious danger. They
had come into power to make peace. They had made it.
The next question was that of the succession of the crown.
Here they neither reflected the general opinion of the
nation nor were agreed amongst themselves. Harley, as
we now know, had flirted with the Jacobites; and Bolingbroke was deep in treasonable plots. The existence of
such plots was a secret to Swift, who indignantly denied
their existence. When King hinted at a possible
danger to Swift from the discovery of St. John's treason,
he indignantly replied that he must have been "a most
false and vile man" to join in anything of the kind.[1] He
professes elsewhere his conviction that there were not at
this period 500 Jacobites in England; and "amongst these
not six of any quality or consequence."[2] Swift's sincerity, here as everywhere, is beyond all suspicion; but
his conviction proves incidentally that he was in the dark
as to the "wheels within wheels"—the backstairs plots,
by which the administration of his friends was hampered
and distracted. With so many causes for jealousy and

[1] Letter to King, Dec. 16th, 1716.
[2] *Inquiry into the Behaviour of the Queen's last Ministry.*

discord, it is no wonder that the political world became a mass of complex intrigue and dispute. The queen, meanwhile, might die at any moment, and some decided course of action become imperatively necessary. Whenever the queen was ill, said Harley, people were at their wits' end; as soon as she recovered they acted as if she were immortal. Yet, though he complained of the general indecision, his own conduct was most hopelessly undecided.

It was in the hopes of pacifying these intrigues that Swift was recalled from Ireland. He plunged into the fight, but not with his old success. Two pamphlets which he published at the end of 1713 are indications of his state of mind. One was an attack upon a wild no-popery shriek emitted by Bishop Burnet, whom he treats, says Johnson, "like one whom he is glad of an opportunity to insult." A man who, like Burnet, is on friendly terms with those who assail the privileges of his order must often expect such treatment from its zealous adherents. Yet the scornful assault, which finds out weak places enough in Burnet's mental rhetoric, is in painful contrast to the dignified argument of earlier pamphlets. The other pamphlet was an incident in a more painful contest. Swift had tried to keep on good terms with Addison and Steele. He had prevented Steele's dismissal from a Commissionership of Stamps. Steele, however, had lost his place of Gazetteer for an attack upon Harley. Swift persuaded Harley to be reconciled to Steele, on condition that Steele should apologize. Addison prevented Steele from making the required submission, "out of mere spite," says Swift, at the thought that Steele should require other help ; rather, we guess, because Addison thought that the submission would savour of party infidelity. A coldness followed ; "all our friendship is over," says Swift of Addison (March 6th, 1711) ; and

though good feeling revived between the principals,
their intimacy ceased. Swift, swept into the ministerial
vortex, pretty well lost sight of Addison; though they
now and then met on civil terms. Addison dined with
Swift and St. John upon April 3rd, 1713, and Swift attended
a rehearsal of *Cato*—the only time when we see him at a
theatre. Meanwhile the ill feeling to Steele remained,
and bore bitter fruit.

Steele and Addison had to a great extent retired from
politics, and during the eventful years 1711-12 were
chiefly occupied in the politically harmless *Spectator*.
But Steele was always ready to find vent for his zeal; and
in 1713 he fell foul of the *Examiner* in the *Guardian*.
Swift had long ceased to write *Examiners* or to be respon-
sible for the conduct of the paper, though he still occasionally inspired the writers. Steele, naturally enough,
supposed Swift to be still at work; and in defending a
daughter of Steele's enemy, Nottingham, not only suggested that Swift was her assailant, but added an insinuation that Swift was an infidel. The imputation
stung Swift to the quick. He had a sensibility to personal attacks, not rare with those who most freely indulge
in them, which was ridiculed by the easy-going Harley.
An attack from an old friend—from a friend whose good
opinion he still valued, though their intimacy had ceased;
from a friend, moreover, whom in spite of their separation
he had tried to protect; and, finally, an attack upon the
tenderest part of his character, irritated him beyond
measure. Some angry letters passed, Steele evidently
regarding Swift as a traitor, and disbelieving his professions of innocence and his claims to active kindness;
whilst Swift felt Steele's ingratitude the more deeply from
the apparent plausibility of the accusation. If Steele was

really unjust and ungenerous, we may admit as a partial
excuse that in such cases the less prosperous combatant has a
kind of right to bitterness.   The quarrel broke out at the
time of Swift's appointment to the deanery. Soon after the
new dean's return to England, Steele was elected member
for Stockbridge, and rushed into political controversy. His
most conspicuous performance was a frothy and pompous
pamphlet called the *Crisis*, intended to rouse alarms as to
French invasion and Jacobite intrigues. Swift took the opportunity to revenge himself upon Steele.   Two pamphlets
—*The importance of the " Guardian" considered*, and *The
Public Spirit of the Whigs* (the latter in answer to the
Crisis)—are fierce attacks upon Steele personally and
politically. Swift's feeling comes out sufficiently in a
remark in the first. He reverses the saying about Cranmer,
and says that he may affirm of Steele, " Do him a good
turn, and he is your enemy for ever."   There is vigorous
writing enough, and effective ridicule of Steele's literary
style and political alarmism.   But it is painfully obvious,
as in the attack upon Burnet, that personal animosity is
now the predominant instead of an auxiliary feeling. Swift
is anxious beyond all things to mortify and humiliate an
antagonist.   And he is in proportion less efficient as a
partizan, though more amusing.   He has, moreover, the
disadvantage of being politically on the defensive.   He is
no longer proclaiming a policy, but endeavouring to disavow the policy attributed to his party.   The wrath which
breaks forth, and the bitter personality with which it is
edged, were far more calculated to irritate his opponents
than to disarm the lookers-on of their suspicions.

Part of the fury was no doubt due to the growing un-
soundness of his political position. Steele in the beginning
of 1714 was expelled from the House for the *Crisis;* and

I

an attack made upon Swift in the House of Lords for
an incidental outburst against the hated Scots in his
reply to the *Crisis*, was only staved off by a manœuvre of
the ministry. Meanwhile Swift was urging the necessity
of union upon men who hated each other more than they
regarded any public cause whatever. Swift at last brought
his two patrons together in Lady Masham's lodgings, and
entreated them to be reconciled. If, he said, they would
agree, all existing mischiefs could be remedied in two
minutes. If they would not, the ministry would be
ruined in two months. Bolingbroke assented : Oxford
characteristically shuffled, said " all would be well," and
asked Swift to dine with him next day. Swift, however,
said that he would not stay to see the inevitable catastrophe. It was his natural instinct to hide his head in
such moments ; his intensely proud and sensitive nature
could not bear to witness the triumph of his enemies, and he
accordingly retired at the end of May, 1714, to the quiet
parsonage of Upper Letcombe in Berkshire. The public
wondered and speculated ; friends wrote letters describing
the scenes which followed, and desiring Swift's help ; and
he read, and walked, and chewed the cud of melancholy
reflection, and thought of stealing away to Ireland. He
wrote, however, a very remarkable pamphlet, giving his
view of the situation, which was not published at the
time ; events went too fast.

Swift's conduct at this critical point is most noteworthy.
The pamphlet (*Free Thoughts upon the Present State of
Affairs*) exactly coincides with all his private and public
utterances. His theory was simple and straightforward.
The existing situation was the culminating result of
Harley's policy of refinement and procrastination. Swift
two years before had written a very able remonstrance

with the October Club, who had sought to push Harley
into decisive measures ; but though he preached patience,
he really sympathized with their motives   Instead of
making a clean sweep of his opponents, Harley had left
many of them in office, either from " refinement "—that
over-subtlety of calculation which Swift thought inferior to
plain common sense, and which, to use his favourite illustration, is like the sharp knife that mangles the paper,
when a plain, blunt paper-knife cuts it properly—or else
from inability to move the Queen, which he had foolishly
allowed to pass for unwillingness, in order to keep up
the appearance of power.   Two things were now to be
done ; first, a clean sweep should be made of all Whigs
and dissenters from office and from the army ; secondly,
the Court of Hanover should be required to break off all
intercourse with the Opposition, on which condition the
heir-presumptive (the infant Prince Frederick) might be
sent over to reside in England.   Briefly, Swift's policy
was a policy of " thorough."   Oxford's vacillations were
the great obstacle, and Oxford was falling before the
alliance of Bolingbroke with Lady Masham.   Bolingbroke
might have turned Swift's policy to the account of the
Jacobites ; but Swift did not take this into account, and
in the *Free Thoughts* he declares his utter disbelief in any
danger to the succession.   What side, then, should he
take ? He sympathized with Bolingbroke's avowed principles.   Bolingbroke was eager for his help, and even
hoped to reconcile him to the red-haired duchess.   But
Swift was bound to Oxford by strong personal affection ;
by an affection which was not diminished even by the fact
that Oxford had procrastinated in the matter of Swift's own
preferment ; and was, at this very moment, annoying him
by delaying to pay the 1000*l.* incurred by his installation

in the deanery. To Oxford he had addressed (Nov. 21, 1713) a letter of consolation upon the death of a daughter, possessing the charm which is given to such letters only by the most genuine sympathy with the feelings of the loser, and by a spontaneous selection of the only safe topic—praise of the lost, equally tender and sincere. Every reference to Oxford is affectionate. When, at the beginning of July, Oxford was hastening to his fall, Swift wrote to him another manly and dignified letter, professing an attachment beyond the reach of external accidents of power and rank. The end came soon. Swift heard that Oxford was about to resign. He wrote at once (July 25, 1714) to propose to accompany him to his country house. Oxford replied two days later in a letter oddly characteristic. He begs Swift to come with him ; "If I have not tired you *tête-à-tête*, fling away so much of your time upon one who loves you ;" and then rather spoils the pathos by a bit of hopeless doggerel. Swift wrote to Miss Vanhomrigh on August 1. "I have been asked," he says, "to join with those people now in power; but I will not do it. I told Lord Oxford I would go with him, when he was out; and now he begs it of me, and I cannot refuse him. I meddle not with his faults, as he was a Minister of State ; but you know his personal kindness to me was excessive ; he distinguished and chose me above all other men, while he was great, and his letter to me the other day was the most moving imaginable."

An intimacy which bore such fruit in time of trial was not one founded upon a servility varnished by self-assertion. No stauncher friend than Swift ever lived. But his fidelity was not to be put to further proof. The day of the letter just quoted was the day of Queen Anne's death. The crash which followed ruined the "people now in

power " as effectually as Oxford.   The party with which
Swift had identified himself, in whose success all his hopes
and ambitions were bound up, was not so much ruined as
annihilated.   " The Earl of Oxford," wrote Bolingbroke
to Swift, " was removed on Tuesday. The Queen died on
Sunday.   What a world is this, and how does fortune
banter us ! "

CHAPTER VI.

STELLA AND VANESSA.

THE final crash of the Tory administration found Swift approaching the end of his forty-seventh year. It found him in his own opinion prematurely aged both in mind and body. His personal prospects and political hopes were crushed. "I have a letter from Dean Swift," says Arbuthnot in September; "he keeps up his noble spirit, and though like a man knocked down, you may behold him still with a stern countenance and aiming a blow at his adversaries." Yet his adversaries knew, and he knew only too well, that such blows as he could now deliver could at most show his wrath without gratifying his revenge. He was disarmed as well as "knocked down." He writes to Bolingbroke from Dublin in despair. "I live a country life in town," he says, "see nobody, and go every day once to prayers, and hope in a few months to grow as stupid as the present situation of affairs will require. Well, after all, parsons are not such bad company, especially when they are under subjection; and I let none but such come near me." Oxford, Bolingbroke, and Ormond were soon in exile or the tower; and a letter to Pope next year gives a sufficient picture of Swift's feelings. "You know," he said, "how well I loved both Lord Oxford and Bolingbroke, and how dear the Duke of

Ormond is to me ; do you imagine I can be easy while their
enemies are endeavouring to take off their heads?—*I
nunc et versus tecum meditare canoros!*" "You are to
understand," he says in conclusion, "that I live in the
corner of a vast unfurnished house ; my family consists of
a steward, a groom, a helper in the stable, a footman, and
an old maid, who are all at board wages, and when I do
not dine abroad or make an entertainment (which last is
very rare), I eat a mutton pie and drink half a pint of
wine ; my amusements are defending my small dominions
against the archbishop, and endeavouring to reduce my
rebellious choir. *Perditur hæc inter misero lux.*" In
another of the dignified letters which show the finest side
of his nature, he offered to join Oxford, whose intrepid
behaviour, he says, "has astonished every one but me, who
know you so well." But he could do nothing beyond
showing sympathy ; and he remained alone asserting his
authority in his ecclesiastical domains, brooding over the
past, and for the time unable to divert his thoughts into
any less distressing channel. Some verses written in
October "in sickness" give a remarkable expression of his
melancholy,—

> 'Tis true—then why should I repine
> To see my life so fast decline ?
> But why obscurely here alone
> Where I am neither loved nor known ?
> My state of health none care to learn,
> My life is here no soul's concern,
> And those with whom I now converse
> Without a tear will tend my hearse.

Yet we might have fancied that his lot would not be so
unbearable. After all, a fall which ends in a deanery
should break no bones. His friends, though hard pressed,

survived; and, lastly, was any one so likely to shed tears
upon his hearse as the woman to whom he was finally
returning? The answer to this question brings us to a
story imperfectly known to us, but of vital importance in
Swift's history.

We have seen in what masterful fashion Swift took
possession of great men. The same imperious temper
shows itself in his relations to women. He required absolute submission. Entrance into the inner circle of his
affections could only be achieved by something like abase-
ment; but all within it became as a part of himself, to be
both cherished and protected without stint. His affectation
of brutality was part of a system. On first meeting Lady
Burlington at her husband's house, he ordered her to sing.
She declined. He replied, "Sing, or I will make you.
Why, madam, I suppose you take me for one of your
English hedge-parsons; sing when I tell you." She burst
into tears and retired. The next time he met her he began,
"Pray, madam, are you as proud and ill-natured as when
I saw you last?" She good-humouredly gave in, and Swift
became her warm friend. Another lady to whom he was
deeply attached was a famous beauty, Anne Long. A
whimsical treaty was drawn up, setting forth that "the
said Dr. Swift, upon the score of his merit and extraordinary qualities, doth claim the sole and undoubted right
that all persons whatever shall make such advance to him
as he pleases to demand, any law, claim, custom, privilege
of sex, beauty, fortune or quality to the contrary notwith-
standing;" and providing that Miss Long shall cease the
contumacy in which she has been abetted by the Vanhomrighs, but be allowed in return, in consideration of her
being "a Lady of the Toast," to give herself the reputation
of being one of Swift's acquaintance. Swift's affection for

Miss Long is touchingly expressed in private papers, and
in a letter written upon her death in retirement and
poverty.   He intends to put up a monument to her
memory, and wrote a notice of her, "to serve her memory,"
and also, as he characteristically adds, to spite the brother
who had neglected her.   Years afterwards he often refers
to the " edict " which he annually issued in England,
commanding all ladies to make him the first advances.
He graciously makes an exception in favour of the Duchess
of Queensberry, though he observes incidentally that he
now hates all people whom he cannot command.   This
humorous assumption, like all Swift's humour, has a
strong element of downright earnest.   He gives whimsical
prominence to a genuine feeling.   He is always acting
the part of despot, and acting it very gravely.   When
he stays at Sir Arthur Acheson's, Lady Acheson becomes
his pupil, and is " severely chid " when she reads wrong.
Mrs. Pendarves, afterwards Mrs. Delany, says in the same
way that Swift calls himself " her master," and corrects
her when she speaks bad English.[1]   He behaved in the
same way to his servants.   Delany tells us that he was
" one of the best masters in the world," paid his servants
the highest rate of wages known, and took great pains
to encourage and help them to save.   But, on engaging
them, he always tested their humility.   One of their duties,
he told them, would be to take turns in cleaning the
scullion's shoes, and if they objected, he sent them about
their business.   He is said to have tested a curate's
docility in the same way by offering him sour wine.   His
dominion was most easily extended over women ; and a
long list might be easily made out of the feminine

[1] *Autobiography*, i. 407.

favourites who at all periods of his life were in more or less intimate relations with this self-appointed sultan. From the wives of peers and the daughters of lord-lieutenants down to Dublin tradeswomen with a taste for rhyming, and even scullerymaids with no tastes at all, a whole hierarchy of female slaves bowed to his rule, and were admitted into higher and lower degrees of favour.

Esther Johnson, or Stella—to give her the name which she did not receive until after the period of the famous journals—was one of the first of these worshippers. As we have seen, he taught her to write, and when he went to Laracor, she accepted the peculiar position already described. We have no direct statement of their mutual feelings before the time of the journal; but one remarkable incident must be noticed. During his stay in England in 1703-4 Swift had some correspondence with a Dublin clergyman named Tisdall. He afterwards regarded Tisdall with a contempt which, for the present, is only half perceptible in some good-humoured raillery. Tisdall's intimacy with "the ladies," Stella and Mrs. Dingley, is one topic, and in the last of Swift's letters we find that Tisdall has actually made an offer for Stella. Swift had replied in a letter (now lost), which Tisdall called unfriendly, unkind, and unaccountable. Swift meets these reproaches coolly, contemptuously, and straightforwardly. He will not affect unconsciousness of Tisdall's meaning. Tisdall obviously takes him for a rival in Stella's affections. Swift replies that he will tell the naked truth. The truth is that "if his fortune and humour served him to think of that state" (marriage) he would prefer Stella to any one on earth. So much, he says, he has declared to Tisdall before. He did not, however, think of his affection as an obstacle to Tisdall's hopes. Tisdall

had been too poor to marry; but the offer of a living has
removed that objection; and Swift undertakes to act what
he has hitherto acted, a friendly though passive part. He
had thought, he declares, that the affair had gone too
far to be broken off; he had always spoken of Tisdall in
friendly terms; "no consideration of my own misfortune
in losing so good a friend and companion as her" shall
prevail upon him to oppose the match, " since it is
held so necessary and convenient a thing for ladies to
marry, and that time takes off from the lustre of virgins
in all other eyes but mine."

The letter must have suggested some doubts to Tisdall.
Swift alleges as his only reasons for not being a rival in
earnest his "humour" and the state of his fortune. The
last obstacle might be removed at any moment. Swift's
prospects, though deferred, were certainly better than
Tisdall's. Unless, therefore, the humour was more in-
surmountable than is often the case, Swift's coolness
was remarkable or ominous. It may be that, as some
have held, there was nothing behind. But another
possibility undoubtedly suggests itself. Stella had received Tisdall's suit so unfavourably that it was now
suspended, and that it finally failed. Stella was corresponding with Swift. It is easy to guess that between
the "unaccountable" letter and the contemptuous letter,
Swift had heard something from Stella, which put him
thoroughly at ease in regard to Tisdall's attentions.

We have no further information until, seven years
afterwards, we reach the *Journal to Stella*, and find ourselves overhearing the "little language." The first
editors scrupled at a full reproduction of what might
strike an unfriendly reader as almost drivelling; and
Mr. Forster reprinted for the first time the omitted

parts of the still accessible letters. The little language is a continuation of Stella's infantile prattle. Certain letters are a cipher for pet names which may be conjectured. Swift calls himself Pdfr, or Podefar, meaning, as Mr. Forster guesses, "Poor, dear Foolish Rogue." Stella, or rather Esther Johnson, is Ppt, say "Poppet." MD, "my dear," means Stella, and sometimes includes Mrs. Dingley. FW means "farewell," or "foolish wenches ;" Lele is taken by Mr. Forster to mean "truly" or "lazy," or "there, there," or to have "other meanings not wholly discoverable." The phrases come in generally by way of leave-taking. "So I got into bed," he says, "to write to MD, MD, for we must always write to MD, MD, MD, awake or asleep ;" and he ends, "Go to bed. Help pdfr. Rove pdfr, MD, MD. Nite darling rogues." Here is another scrap, "I assure oo it im vely late now ; but zis goes to-morrow ; and I must have time to converse with own deerichar MD. Nite de deer Sollahs." One more leave-taking may be enough. " Farewell, dearest hearts and souls, MD. Farewell, MD, MD, MD. FW, FW, FW. ME, ME. Lele, Lele, Lele, Sollahs, Lele."

The reference to the Golden Farmer already noted is in the words, " I warrant oo don't remember the Golden Farmer neither, Figgarkick Solly," and I will venture to a guess at what Mr. Forster pronounces to be inexplicable.[2] May not Solly be the same as " Sollah," generally interpreted by the editors as " sirrah ;" and " Figgarkick " possibly be the same as Pilgarlick, a phrase which he elsewhere applies to Stella,[3] and which the dictionaries say means " poor, deserted creature " ?

[2] *Foster,* p. 108.
[3] Oct. 20th, 1711. The last use I have observed of this word is

Swift says that as he writes his language he "makes up his mouth just as if he was speaking it." It fits the affectionate caresses in which he is always indulging. Nothing, indeed, can be more charming than the playful little prattle which occasionally interrupts the gossip and the sharp utterances of hope or resentment. In the snatches of leisure, late at night or before he has got up in the morning, he delights in an imaginary chat; for a few minutes of little fondling talk help him to forget his worries, and anticipate the happiness of reunion. He caresses her letters, as he cannot touch her hand. " And now let us come and see what this saucy, dear letter of MD says. Come out, letter, come out from between the sheets; here it is underneath, and it will not come out. Come out again, I says; so there. Here it is. What says Pdf to me, pray? says it. Come and let me answer for you to your ladies. Hold up your head then like a good letter." And so he begins a little talk, and prays that they may be never separated again for ten days, whilst he lives. Then he follows their movements in Dublin in passages which give some lively little pictures of their old habits. "And where will you go to-day? for I cannot be with you for the ladies." [He is off sight-seeing to the Tower and Bedlam with Lady Kerry and a friend.] "It is a rainy, ugly day; I would have you send for Wales, and go to the deans; but do not play small games when you lose. You will be ruined by Manilio, Basto, the queen, and two small trumps in red. I confess it is a good hand against the player. But, then, there are Spadilio, Punto, the king, strong trumps against you, which with one rump more are three tricks ten ace;

in a letter of Carlyle's, Nov. 7th, 1824. " Strange pilgarlic-looking figures." Froude's *Life of Carlyle*, i. 247.

for suppose you play your Manilio—O, silly, how I prate
and cannot get away from MD in a morning. Go, get
you gone, dear naughty girls, and let me rise." He
delights again in turning to account his queer talent for
making impromptu proverbs,—

> Be you lords or be you earls,
> You must write to naughty girls.

Or again,—

> Mr. White and Mr. Red
> Write to M.D. when abed :
> Mr. Black and Mr. Brown
> Write to M.D. when you are down :
> Mr. Oak and Mr. Willow
> Write to M.D. on your pillow.

And here is one more for the end of the year,—

> Would you answer M.D.'s letter
> On New Year's Day you will do it better :
> For when the year with M.D. 'gins
> It without M.D never 'lins.

"These proverbs," he explains, "have always old words
in them ; *lin* is leave off."

> But if on new year you write nones
> M.D. then will bang your bones.

Reading these fond triflings we feel even now as though
we were unjustifiably prying into the writer's confidence.
What are we to say to them ? We might simply say that
the tender playfulness is charming ; and that it is delightful to find the stern gladiator turning from party-warfare
to soothe his wearied soul with these tender caresses.
There is but one drawback. Macaulay imitates some of
this prattle in his charming letters to his younger sister,

and there we can accept it without difficulty. But Stella
was not Swift's younger sister. She was a beautiful and
clever woman of thirty, when he was in the prime of his
powers at forty-four. If Tisdall could have seen the journal
he would have ceased to call Swift "unaccountable." Did
all this caressing suggest nothing to Stella? Swift does not
write as an avowed lover; Dingley serves as a chaperone
even in these intimate confidences; and yet a word or two
escapes which certainly reads like something more than
fraternal affection. He apologizes (May 23, 1711) for not
returning; "I will say no more, but beg you to be easy
till fortune takes her course, and to believe that MD's
felicity is the great goal I aim at in all my pursuits." If
such words addressed under such circumstances did not
mean "I hope to make you my wife as soon as I get a
deanery," there must have been some distinct understanding to limit their force.

But another character enters the drama. Mrs. Vanhomrigh,[4] a widow rich enough to mix in good society, was
living in London with two sons and two daughters, and
made Swift's acquaintance in 1708. Her eldest daughter,
Hester, was then seventeen, or about ten years younger
than Stella. When Swift returned to London in 1710, he
took lodgings close to the Vanhomrighs, and became an
intimate of the family. In the daily reports of his dinner,
the name Van occurs more frequently than any other.
Dinner, let us observe in passing, had not then so much
as now the character of a solemn religious rite, implying a
formal invitation. The ordinary hour was three (though
Harley with his usual procrastination often failed to sit
down till six), and Swift, when not pre-engaged, looked

[4] Lord Orrery instructs us to pronounce this name Vanummery.

in at Court or elsewhere in search of an invitation. He
seldom failed : and when nobody else offered he frequently
went to the "Vans." The name of the daughter is only
mentioned two or three times ; whilst it is perhaps a
suspicious circumstance that he very often makes a quasi-
apology for his dining-place. " I was so lazy I dined
where my new gown was, at Mrs. Vanhomrigh's," he
says, in May, 1711 ; and a day or two later explains that
he keeps his " best gown and periwig " there whilst he is
lodging at Chelsea, and often dines there " out of mere
listlessness." The phrase may not have been consciously
insincere ; but Swift was drifting into an intimacy which
Stella could hardly approve, and, if she desired Swift's
love, would regard as ominous. When Swift took
possession of his deanery, he revealed his depression to
Miss Vanhomrigh, who about this time took the title
Vanessa ; and Vanessa again received his confidences from
Letcombe. A full account of their relations is given in
the remarkable poem called *Cadenus and Vanessa*, less
remarkable, indeed, as a poem than as an autobiographical
document. It is singularly characteristic of Swift that
we can use what, for want of a better classification, must
be called a love poem, as though it were an affidavit in
a law-suit. Most men would feel some awkwardness in
hinting at sentiments conveyed by Swift in the most
downright terms ; to turn them into a poem would seem
preposterous. Swift's poetry, however, is always plain
matter of fact, and we may read *Cadenus* (which means of
course *Decanus*) *and Vanessa* as Swift's deliberate and
palpably sincere account of his own state of mind.
Omitting a superfluous framework of mythology in the contemporary taste, we have a plain story of the relations of
this new Heloïse and Abelard. Vanessa, he tells us, united

masculine accomplishments to feminine grace ; the fashion-
able fops (I use Swift's own words as much as possible) who
tried to entertain her with the tattle of the day, stared
when she replied by applications of Plutarch's morals ; the
ladies from the purlieus of St. James's found her reading
Montaigne at her toilet, and were amazed by her ignorance
of the fashions.   Both were scandalized at the waste of
such charms and talents due to the want of so called
knowledge of the world.   Meanwhile, Vanessa, not yet
twenty, met and straightway admired Cadenus, though
his eyes were dim with study and his health decayed.
He had grown old in politics and wit ; was caressed by
ministers ; dreaded and hated by half mankind, and had
forgotten the arts by which he had once charmed ladies,
though merely for amusement and to show his wit.[5]   He
did not understand what was love ; he behaved to Vanessa
as a father might behave to a daughter ;

> That innocent delight he took
> To see the virgin mind her book
> Was but the master's secret joy
> In school to hear the finest boy.

Vanessa, once the quickest of learners, grew distracted.
He apologized for having bored her by his pedantry, and
offered a last adieu.   She then startled him by a confession.   He had taught her, she said, that virtue should
never be afraid of disclosures ; that noble minds were
above common maxims (just what he had said to Varina),
and she therefore told him frankly that his lessons, aimed
at her head, had reached her heart.   Cadenus was utterly
taken aback.   Her words were too plain to be in jest.

[5] This simply repeats what he says in his first published letters
about his flirtations at Leicester.

K

He was conscious of having never for a moment meant to
be other than a teacher. Yet every one would suspect
him of intentions to win her heart and her five thousand
pounds. He tried not to take things seriously. Vanessa,
however, became eloquent. She said that he had taught
her to love great men through their books ; why should
she not love the living reality ? Cadenus was flattered
and half converted. He had never heard her talk so
well, and admitted that she had a most unfailing judgment and discerning head. He still maintained that his
dignity and age put love out of the question, but he
offered in return as much friendship as she pleased. She
replies that she will now become tutor and teach him the
lesson which he is so slow to learn. But—and here the
revelation ends—

> But what success Vanessa met
> Is to the world a secret yet.[6]

Vanessa loved Swift ; and Swift, it seems, allowed
himself to be loved. One phrase in a letter written to
him during his stay at Dublin, in 1713, suggests the
only hint of jealousy. If you are happy, she says, "it is
ill-natured of you not to tell me so, except 'tis what is
inconsistent with mine." Soon after Swift's final retirement, to Ireland, Mrs. Vanhomrigh died ; her husband
had left a small property at Celbridge. One son was
dead ; the other behaved badly to his sisters ; the
daughters were for a time in money difficulties, and it

---

[6] The passage which contains this line was said by Orrery to
cast an unmanly insinuation against Vanessa's virtue. As the
accusation has been repeated, it is perhaps right to say that one
fact sufficiently disproves its possibility. The poem was intended
for Vanessa alone ; and would never have appeared had it not been
published after her death by her own direction.

became convenient for them to retire to Ireland, where
Vanessa ultimately settled at Celbridge. The two
women who worshipped Swift were thus almost in
presence of each other. The situation almost suggests
comedy ; but unfortunately it was to take a most tragical
and still partly mysterious development.

The fragmentary correspondence between Swift and
Vanessa establishes certain facts. Their intercourse was
subject to restraints. He begs her, when he is starting
for Dublin, to get her letters directed by some other hand,
and to write nothing that may not be seen, for fear of
"inconveniences." The post-office clerk surely would not be
more attracted by Vanessa's hand than by that of such a
man as Lewis, a subordinate of Harley's who had formerly
forwarded her letters. He adds that if she comes to
Ireland, he will see her very seldom. "It is not a place
for freedom, but everything is known in a week and
magnified a hundred times." Poor Vanessa soon finds
the truth of this. She complains that she is amongst
"strange prying deceitful people ;" that he flies her and
will give no reason except that they are amongst fools
and must submit. His reproofs are terrible to her. "If
you continue to treat me as you do," she says soon after,
"you will not be made uneasy by me long." She would
rather have borne the rack than those "killing, killing
words" of his. She writes instead of speaking, because
when she ventures to complain in person "you are angry,
and there is something in your look so awful that it shakes
me dumb"—a memorable phrase in days soon to come.
She protests that she says as little as she can. If he knew
what she thought, he must be moved. The letter containing
these phrases is dated 1714, and there are but a few scraps
till 1720 ; we gather that Vanessa submitted partly to the

necessities of the situation : and that this extreme tension
was often relaxed. Yet she plainly could not resign herself
or suppress her passion. Two letters in 1720 are painfully vehement. He has not seen her for ten-long weeks,
she says in her first, and she has only had one letter
and one little note with an excuse. She will sink under
his "prodigious neglect." Time or accident cannot lessen
her inexpressible passion. "Put my passion under the
utmost restraint; send me as distant from you as the
earth will allow, yet you cannot banish those charming
ideas which will stick by me, whilst I have the use of
memory. Nor is the love I bear you only seated in my
soul, for there is not a single atom of my frame that is
not blended with it." She thinks him changed, and
entreats him not to suffer her to "live a life like a
languishing death, which is the only life I can lead, if
you have lost any of your tenderness for me." The
following letter is even more passionate. She passes
days in sighing and nights in watching and thinking of
one who thinks not of her. She was born with "violent
passions, which terminate all in one, that inexpressible
passion I have for you." If she could guess at his
thoughts, which is impossible ("for never any one living
thought like you") she would guess that he wishes her
"religious"—that she might pay her devotions to heaven.
"But that should not spare you, for was I an enthu-
siast, still you'd be the deity I should worship." "What
marks are there of a deity but what you are to be known
by—you are (at?) present everywhere; your dear image
is always before my eyes. Sometimes you strike me
with that prodigious awe, I tremble with fear ; at other
times a charming compassion shines through your countenance, which moves my soul. Is it not more reasonable

to adore a radiant form one has seen, than one only
described ?" [7]

The man who received such letters from a woman
whom he at least admired and esteemed, who felt that
to respond was to administer poison, and to fail to
respond was to inflict the severest pangs, must have been
in the cruellest of dilemmas. Swift, we cannot doubt,
was grieved and perplexed. His letters imply embarrass-
ment ; and, for the most part, take a lighter tone ; he
suggests his universal panacea of exercise : tells her to fly
from the spleen instead of courting it; to read diverting
books, and so forth ; advice more judicious probably than
comforting. There are, however, some passages of a
different tendency. There is a mutual understanding to
use certain catch-words, which recall the "little language." He wishes that her letters were as hard to read
as his, in case of accident. "A stroke thus . . . signifies
everything that may be said to Cad, at the beginning and
conclusion." And she uses this written caress, and signs
herself—his own "Skinage." There are certain "questions," to which reference is occasionally made ; a kind of
catechism, it seems, which he was expected to address to
himself at intervals, and the nature of which must be
conjectured. He proposes to continue the Cadenus and
Vanessa—a proposal which makes her happy beyond "expression,"—and delights her by recalling a number of
available incidents. He recurs to them in his last letter,
and bids her "go over the scenes of Windsor, Cleveland
Row, Rider Street, St. James's Street, Kensington, the

[7] Compare Pope's *Eloisa* to *Abelard* which appeared in 1717.
If Vanessa had read it, she might almost be suspected of borrowing ; but her phrases seem to be too genuine to justify the
hypothesis.

Shrubbery, the Colonel in France, &c. Cad thinks
often of these, especially on horseback,[8] as I am assured."
This prosaic list of names recall, as we find, various old
meetings. And, finally, one letter contains an avowal of
a singular kind. " Soyez assurée," he says, after advising
her " to quit this scoundrel island," "que jamais personne
du monde a èté aimée, honorée, estimée, adorée par votre
ami que vous." It seems as though he were compelled to
throw her just a crumb of comfort here : but, in the same
breath, he has begged her to leave him for ever.

If Vanessa was ready to accept a " gown of forty-four,"
to overlook his infirmities in consideration of his fame,
why should Swift have refused ? Why condemn her to
undergo this " languishing death,"—a long agony of unre-
quited passion ? One answer is suggested by the report
that Swift was secretly married to Stella in 1716. The
fact is not proved, nor disproved :[9] nor, to my mind, is

[8] Scott appropriately'quotes Hotspur. The phrase is apparently
a hint at Swift's usual recipe of exercise.

[9] I cannot here discuss the evidence. The original statements
are in *Orrery*, p. 22 &c.; *Delany*, p. 52 ; *Dean Swift*, p. 93 ; *Sheridan*,
p. 282 ; *Monck Berkeley*, p. xxxvi. Scott accepted the marriage,
and the evidence upon which he relied was criticized by Monck
Mason, p. 297, &c. Monck Mason makes some good points, and
especially diminishes the value of the testimony of Bishop Berkeley, showing by dates that he could not have heard the story, as
his grandson affirms, from Bishop Ashe, who is said to have performed the ceremony. It probably came, however, from Berkeley,
who,we may add, was tutor to Ashe's son, and had special reasons
for interest in the story. On the whole, the argument for the
marriage comes to this : that it was commonly reported by the
end of Swift's life, that it was certainly believed by his intimate
friend Delany, in all probability by the elder Sheridan and by
Mrs. Whiteway. Mrs. Sican, who told the story to Sheridan, seems
also to be a good witness. On the other hand, Dr. Lyon, a clergyman who was one of Swift's guardians in his imbecility, says that

the question of its truth of much importance. The ceremony, if performed, was nothing but a ceremony. The only rational explanation of the fact, if it be taken for a fact, must be that Swift, having resolved not to marry, gave Stella this security that he would, at least, marry no one else. Though his anxiety to hide the connexion with Vanessa may only mean a dread of idle tongues, it is at least highly probable that Stella was the person from whom he specially desired to keep it. Yet his poetical addresses to Stella upon her birthday (of which the first is dated 1719, ånd the last 1727) are clearly not the addresses of a lover. Both in form and substance they are even pointedly intended to express friendship instead of love. They read like an expansion of his avowal to Tisdall, that her charms for him, though for no one else, could not be diminished by her growing old without marriage. He addresses her with blunt affection, and tells her plainly of her growing size and waning beauty ; comments even upon her defects of temper, and seems expressly to deny that he loved her in the usual way.

> Thou, Stella, wert no longer young
> When first for thee my harp I strung,
> Without one word of Cupid's darts
> Of killing eyes and bleeding hearts ;
> With friendship and esteem possess'd
> I ne'er admitted love a guest.

We may almost say that he harps upon the theme of " friendship and esteem." His gratitude for her care of him is pathetically expressed ; he admires her with the

it was denied by Mrs. Dingley and by Mrs. Brent, Swift's old housekeeper, and by Stella's executors. The evidence seems to me very indecisive. Much of it may be dismissed as mere gossip, but a certain probability remains.

devotion of a brother for the kindest of sisters ; his plain
prosaic lines become poetical, or perhaps something better ;
but there is an absence of the lover's strain which is only
not, if not, ostentatious.

The connexion with Stella, whatever its nature, gives
the most intelligible explanation of his keeping Vanessa
at a distance.   A collision between his two slaves might
be disastrous.   And, as the story goes (for we are everywhere upon uncertain ground), it came.   In 1721 poor
Vanessa had lost her only sister,[1] and companion : her
brothers were already dead, and, in her solitude, she would
naturally be more than ever eager for Swift's kindness.
At last, in 1723, she wrote (it is said) a letter to Stella, and
asked whether she was Swift's wife.[2]   Stella replied that she
was, and forwarded Vanessa's letter to Swift.   How Swift
could resent an attempt to force his wishes, has been seen
in the letter to Varina.   He rode in a fury to Celbridge.
His countenance, says Orrery, could be terribly expressive of the sterner passions.   Prominent eyes—" azure as
the heavens " (says Pope)—arched by bushy black eye-
brows, could glare, we can believe from his portraits, with
the green fury of a cat's.   Vanessa had spoken of the
" something awful in his looks," and of his killing words.
He now entered her room, silent with rage, threw down
her letter on the table and rode off.   He had struck
Vanessa's death-blow.   She died soon afterwards, but
lived long enough to revoke a will made in favour of
Swift, and leave her money between Judge Marshal and
the famous Bishop Berkeley.   Berkeley, it seems, had
only seen her once in his life.

[1] *Monck Mason*, p. 310, note.
[2] This is Sheridan's story.   Orrery speaks of the letter as
written to Swift himself.

The story of the last fatal interview has been denied.
Vanessa's death, though she was under thirty-five, is less
surprising when we remember that her younger sister and
both her brothers had died before her ; and that her
health had always been weak, and her life for some time a
languishing death.   That there was in any case a terribly
tragic climax to the half-written romance of *Cadenus and
Vanessa* is certain.   Vanessa requested that the poem
and the letters might be published by her executors.
Berkeley suppressed the letters for the time ; and they
were not published in full until Scott's edition of Swift's
works.

Whatever the facts, Swift had reasons enough for bitter
regret if not for deep remorse.   He retired to hide his
head in some unknown retreat ; absolute seclusion was
the only solace to his gloomy, wounded spirit.   After two
months he returned to resume his retired habits.   A period,
followed, as we shall see in the next chapter, of fierce
political excitement.   For a time too he had a vague
hope of escaping from his exile.   An astonishing literary
success increased his reputation.   But another misfortune approached which crushed all hope of happiness in
life.

In 1726 Swift at last revisited England.   He writes
in July that he has for two months been anxious about
Stella's health, and as usual feared the worst.   He has seen
through the disguises of a letter from Mrs. Dingley.   His
heart is so sunk that he will never be the same man again,
but drag on a wretched life till it pleases God to call him
away.   Then in an agony of distress he contemplates her
death ; he says that he could not bear to be present ; he
should be a trouble to her, and the greatest torment to
himself.   He forces himself to add that her death must

not take place at the deanery.   He will not return to find
her just dead or dying.   "Nothing but extremity could
make me so familiar with those terrible words applied to
so dear a friend."   "I think," he says in another letter,
"that there is not a greater folly than that of entering
into too strict a partnership or friendship with the loss
of which a man must be absolutely miserable; but
especially [when the loss occurs] at an age when it is too
late to engage in a new friendship."   The morbid feeling
which could withhold a man from attending a friend's
deathbed, or allow him to regret the affection to which his
pain was due, is but too characteristic of Swift's egoistic
attachments.   Yet we forgive the rash phrase, when we
read his passionate expressions of agony.   Swift returned
to Ireland in the autumn, and Stella struggled through the
winter.   He was again in England in the following summer; and for a time in better spirits.   But once more the
news comes that Stella is probably on her deathbed; and
he replies in letters which we read as we listen to groans
of a man in sorest agony.   He keeps one letter for an
hour before daring to open it.   He does not wish to live
to see the loss of the person for whose sake alone life was
worth preserving.   "What have I to do in the world?   I
never was in such agonies as when I received your letter,
and had it in my pocket.   I am able to hold up my sorry
head no longer."   In another distracted letter, he repeats
in Latin the desire that Stella shall not die in the deanery,
for fear of malignant misinterpretations.   If any marriage
had taken place, the desire to conceal it had become a
rooted passion.

Swift returned to Ireland to find Stella still living.   It
is said that in the last period of her life Swift offered to
make the marriage public, and that she declined, saying

that it was now too late.[3] She lingered till January 28,
1728. He sat down the same night to write a few
scattered reminiscences. He breaks down; and writes
again during the funeral, which he is too ill to attend.
The fragmentary notes give us the most authentic account
of Stella, and show, at least, what she appeared in the eyes
of her lifelong friend and protector. We may believe
that she was intelligent and charming ; as we can be certain that Swift loved her in every sense but one. A lock
of her hair was preserved in an envelope in which he had
written one of those vivid phrases by which he still lives
in our memory : " *Only a woman's hair.*" What does it
mean ? Our interpretation will depend partly upon what
we can see ourselves in a lock of hair. But I think that
any one who judges Swift fairly will read in those four
words the most intense utterance of tender affection, and
of pathetic yearning for the irrevocable past strangely
blended with a bitterness springing not from remorse, but
indignation at the cruel tragi-comedy of life. The
destinies laugh at us whilst they torture us ; they make
cruel scourges of trifles, and extract the bitterest passion
from our best affections.

Swift was left alone. Before we pass on we must
briefly touch the problems of this strange history. It was a
natural guess that some mysterious cause condemned Swift
to his loneliness. A story is told by Scott (on poor evidence) that Delany went to Archbishop King's library
about the time of the supposed marriage. As he entered

---

[3] Scott heard this from Mrs. Whiteway's grandson. Sheridan
tells the story as though Stella had begged for publicity, and Swift
cruelly refused. Delany's statement (p. 56), which agrees with
Mrs. Whiteway's, appears to be on good authority, and, if true,
proves the reality of the marriage.

Swift rushed out with a distracted countenance. King was in tears, and said to Delany, " You have just met the most unhappy man on earth ; but on the subject of his wretchedness you must never ask a question." This has been connected with a guess made by somebody that Swift had discovered Stella to be his natural sister. It can be shown conclusively that this is impossible ; and the story must be left as picturesque but too hopelessly vague to gratify any inference whatever. We know without it that Swift was unhappy ; but we know nothing of any definite cause.

Another view is that there is no mystery. Swift, it is said, retained through life the position of Stella's "guide, philosopher and friend," and was never anything more. Stella's address to Swift (on his birthday, 1721), may be taken to confirm this theory. It says with a plainness like his own that he had taught her to despise beauty and hold her empire by virtue and sense. Yet the theory is in itself strange. The less love entered into Swift's relations to Stella, the more difficult to explain his behaviour to Vanessa. If he regarded Stella only as a daughter or a younger sister, and she returned the same feeling, he had no reason for making any mystery about the woman who would not in that case be a rival. If, again, we accept this view, we naturally ask why Swift "never admitted love a guest." He simply continued, it is suggested, to behave as teacher to pupil. He thought of her when she was a woman as he had thought of her when she was a child of eight years old. But it is singular that a man should be able to preserve such a relation. It is quite true that a connexion of this kind may blind a man to its probable consequences ; but it is contrary to ordinary experience that

it should render the consequences less probable.   The
relation might explain why Swift should be off his guard ;
but could hardly act as a safeguard.   An ordinary man
who was on such terms with a beautiful girl as are revealed
in the *Journal to Stella* would have ended by falling in
love with her.   Why did not Swift ?   We can only reply
by remembering the " coldness " of temper to which he
refers in his first letter : and his assertion that he did not
understand love, and that his frequent flirtations never
meant more than a desire for distraction.   The affair with
Varina is an exception : but there are grounds for holding that Swift was constitutionally indisposed to the
passion of love.   The absence of any traces of such a
passion from writings conspicuous for their amazing sincerity, and (it is added) for their freedoms of another
kind, has been often noticed as a confirmation of this
hypothesis.   Yet it must be said that Swift could be
strictly reticent about his strongest feelings—and was
specially cautious, for whatever reason, in regard to his
relation with Stella.[4]

If Swift constitutionally differed from other   men,
we have some explanation of his strange conduct.   But
we must take into account other circumstances.   Swift
had very obvious motives for not marrying.   In the first
place, he gradually became almost a monomaniac upon
the question of money.   His hatred of wasting a penny
unnecessarily began at Trinity College, and is prominent
in all his letters and journals.   It coloured even his
politics, for a conviction that the nation was hopelessly
ruined is one of his strongest prejudices.   He kept
accounts down to halfpence, and rejoices at every saving

[4] Besides Scott's remarks (see v. of his life) see Orrery, *Letter*
10 ; *Deane Swift*, p. 93, *Sheridan*, p. 297.

of a shilling. The passion was not the vulgar desire for
wealth of the ordinary miser. It sprang from the conviction stored up in all his aspirations that money meant
independence. " Wealth," he says, " is liberty ; and
liberty is a blessing fittest for a philosopher—and Gay
is a slave just by two thousand pounds too little." [5] Gay
was a duchess's lapdog : Swift, with all his troubles, at
least a free man. Like all Swift's prejudices, this became
a fixed idea which was always gathering strength. He did
not love money for its own sake. He was even magnificent in his generosity. He scorned to receive money for
his writings ; he abandoned the profit to his printers in com-
pensation for the risks they ran, or gave it to his friends.
His charity was splendid relatively to his means. In
later years he lived on a third of his income, gave away
a third, and saved the remaining third for his posthumous
charity,[6]—and posthumous charity which involves present saving is charity of the most unquestionable kind.
His principle was that by reducing his expenditure to the
lowest possible point, he secured his independence and
could then make a generous use of the remainder. Until
he had received his deanery, however, he could only
make both ends meet. Marriage would therefore have
meant poverty, probably dependence, and the complete
sacrifice of his ambition.

If under these circumstances Swift had become engaged
to Stella upon Temple's death, he would have been
doing what was regularly done by fellows of colleges
under the old system. There is, however, no trace of
such an engagement. It would be in keeping with Swift's
character, if we should suppose that he shrank from the

[5] *Letter to Pope*, July 16th, 1728.   [6] *Sheridan*, p. 23.

bondage of an engagement ; that he designed to marry
Stella as soon as he should achieve a satisfactory position,
and meanwhile trusted to his influence over her, and
thought that he was doing her justice by leaving her at
liberty to marry if she chose.   The close connexion must
have been injurious to Stella's prospects of a match ; but
it continued only by her choice.   If this were in fact the
case, it is still easy to understand why Swift did not marry
upon becoming dean.   He felt himself, I have said, to be
a broken man.   His prospects were ruined, and his health
precarious.   This last fact requires to be remembered in
every estimate of Swift's character.   His life was passed
under a Damocles' sword.   He suffered from a distressing
illness which he attributed to an indigestion produced by
an over-consumption of fruit at Temple's when he was a
little over twenty-one.   The main symptoms were a giddiness, which frequently attacked him, and was accompanied by deafness.   It is quite recently that the true
nature of the complaint has been identified.   Dr. Bucknill[7] seems to prove that the symptoms are those of
"Labyrinthine vertigo," or Ménière's disease, so called
because discovered by Ménière in 1861.   The references
to his sufferings, brought together by Sir William Wilde
in 1849,[8] are frequent in all his writings.   It tormented
him for days, weeks, and months, gradually becoming
more permanent in later years.   In 1731 he tells Gay
that his giddiness attacks him constantly, though it is less
violent than of old ; and in 1736 he says that it is continual.   From a much earlier period it had alarmed and
distressed him.   Some pathetic entries are given by Mr.
Forster from one of his note-books :—" Dec. 5 (1708).

[7] *Brain* for Jan., 1882.
[8] *Closing Years of Dean Swift's Life.*

—Horribly sick. 12th.—Much better, thank God and
M.D.'s prayers. . . . April 2nd (1709).—Small giddy fit
and swimming in the head. M.D. and God help me. . . .
July, 1710.—Terrible fit. God knows what may be the
event. Better towards the end." The terrible anxiety,
always in the background, must count for much in Swift's
gloomy despondency. Though he seems always to have
spoken of the fruit as the cause, he must have had misgivings as to the nature and result. Dr. Bucknill tells us
that it was not necessarily connected with the disease of
the brain, which ultimately came upon him ; but he may
well have thought that this disorder of the head was
prophetic of such an end. It was probably in 1717 that
he said to Young of the *Night Thoughts*, "I shall be
like that tree ; I shall die at the top." A man haunted
perpetually by such forebodings might well think that
marriage was not for him. In *Cadenus and Vanessa* he
insists upon his declining years with an emphasis which
seems excessive even from a man of forty-four (in 1713 he
was really forty-five) to a girl of twenty. In a singular
poem called the *Progress of Marriage* he treats the supposed case of a divine of fifty-two marrying a lively girl of
fashion, and speaks with his usual plainness of the probable consequences of such folly. We cannot doubt that
here as elsewhere he is thinking of himself. He was fifty-
two when receiving the passionate love-letters of Vanessa ;
and the poem seems to be specially significant.

This is one of those cases in which we feel that even
biographers are not omniscient ; and I must leave it to my
readers to choose their own theory, only suggesting that
readers too are fallible. But we may still ask what judgment
is to be passed upon Swift's conduct. Both Stella and
Vanessa suffered from coming within the sphere of Swift's

imperious attraction. Stella enjoyed his friendship through
her life at the cost of a partial isolation from ordinary domestic happiness. She might and probably did regard his
friendship as a full equivalent for the sacrifice. It is one of
the cases in which, if the actors be our contemporaries, we
hold that outsiders are incompetent to form a judgment,
as none but the principals can really know the facts. Is
it better to be the most intimate friend of a man of genius
or the wife of a commonplace Tisdall? If Stella chose,
and chose freely, it is hard to say that she was mistaken,
or to blame Swift for a fascination which he could not
but exercise. The tragedy of Vanessa suggests rather
different reflections. Swift's duty was plain. Granting
what seems to be probable, that Vanessa's passion took
him by surprise, and that he thought himself disqualified
for marriage by infirmity and weariness of life, he should
have made his decision perfectly plain. He should have
forbidden any clandestine relations. Furtive caresses—
even on paper, understandings to carry on a private
correspondence, fond references to old meetings, were
obviously calculated to encourage her passion. He should
not only have pronounced it to be hopeless, but made her,
at whatever cost, recognize the hopelessness. This is
where Swift's strength seems to have failed him. He was
not intentionally cruel; he could not foresee the fatal
event; he tried to put her aside, and he felt the " shame,
disappointment, grief, surprise," of which he speaks on
the avowal of her love. He gave her the most judicious
advice, and tried to persuade her to accept it. But he did
not make it effectual. He shrank from inflicting pain
upon her and upon himself. He could not deprive himself of the sympathy which soothed his gloomy melancholy. His affection was never free from the egoistic

L

element which prevented him from acting unequivocally
as an impartial spectator would have advised him to act,
or as he would have advised another to act in a similar
case.   And therefore when the crisis came the very
strength of his affection produced an explosion of selfish
wrath; and he escaped from the intolerable position by
striking down the woman whom he loved, and whose love
for him had become a burden.   The wrath was not the
less fatal because it was half composed of remorse, and the
energy of the explosion proportioned to the strength of the
feeling which had held it in check.

CHAPTER VII.

In one of Scott's finest novels, the old Cameronian preacher, who had been left for dead by Claverhouse's troopers, suddenly rises to confront his conquerors, and spends his last breath in denouncing the oppressors of the saints. Even such an apparition was Jonathan Swift to comfortable Whigs who were flourishing in the place of Harley and St. John, when, after ten years' quiescence, he suddenly stepped into the political arena. After the first crushing fall he had abandoned partial hope, and contented himself with establishing supremacy in his chapter. But undying wrath smouldered in his breast till time came for an outburst.

No man had ever learnt more thoroughly the lesson, "put not your faith in princes;" or had been impressed with a lower estimate of the wisdom displayed by the rulers of the world. He had been behind the scenes, and knew that the wisdom of great ministers meant just enough cunning to court the ruin which a little common sense would have avoided. Corruption was at the prow and folly at the helm. The selfish ring which he had denounced so fiercely had triumphed. It had triumphed, as he held, by flattering the new dynasty, hood-winking the nation, and maligning its antagonists. The

cynical theory of politics was not for him, as for some
comfortable cynics, an abstract proposition, which mattered
very little to a sensible man ; but was embodied in the
bitter wrath with which he regarded his triumphant
adversaries. Pessimism is perfectly compatible with
bland enjoyment of the good things in a bad world ; but
Swift's pessimism was not of this type. It meant
energetic hatred of definite things and people who were
always before him.

With this feeling, he had come to Ireland ; and Ireland
—I am speaking of a century and a half ago—was the
opprobrium of English statesmanship. There Swift had
(or thought he had) always before him a concrete example
of the basest form of tyranny. By Ireland, I have said,
Swift meant, in the first place, the English in Ireland.
In the last years of his sanity he protested indignantly against the confusion between the " savage old
Irish," and the English gentry who, he said, were much
better bred, spoke better English, and were more civilized
than the inhabitants of many English counties.[1] He
retained to the end of his life his antipathy to the Scotch
colonists. He opposed their demand for political equality
as fiercely in the last as in his first political utterances.
He contrasted them unfavourably[2] with the Catholics, who
had indeed been driven to revolt by massacre and confis-
cation under Puritan rule, but who were now, he declared,
" true Whigs, in the best and most proper sense of the
word," and thoroughly loyal to the house of Hanover.
Had there been a danger of a Catholic revolt, Swift's
feelings might have been different ; but he always held,
that they were " as inconsiderable as the women and

[1] Letter to Pope, July 13th, 1737.
[2] *Catholic Reasons for Repealing the Test.*

children," mere " hewers of wood and drawers of water,"
" out of all capacity of doing any mischief, if they were
ever so well inclined." ³ Looking at them in this way,
he felt a sincere compassion for their misery and a bitter
resentment against their oppressors. The English, he
said, in a remarkable letter,⁴ should be ashamed of their
reproaches of Irish dulness, ignorance and cowardice.
Those defects were the products of slavery. He declared
that the poor cottagers had " a much better natural taste
for good sense, humour and raillery, than ever I observed
among people of the like sort in England. But the
millions of oppressions they lie under, the tyranny of their
landlords, the ridiculous zeal of their priests, and the
misery of the whole nation have been enough to damp
the best spirits under the sun." Such a view is now
commonplace enough. It was then a heresy to English
statesmen, who thought that nobody but a Papist or a
Jacobite could object to the tyranny of Whigs.

Swift's diagnosis of the chronic Irish disease was
thoroughly political. He considered that Irish misery
sprang from the subjection to a government not intentionally cruel, but absolutely selfish ; to which the Irish
revenue meant so much convenient political plunder,
and which acted on the principle quoted from Cowley,
that the happiness of Ireland should not weigh against the
" least conveniency " of England. He summed up his views
in a remarkable letter,⁵ to be presently mentioned, the
substance of which had been orally communicated to Walpole. He said to Walpole, as he said in every published,
utterance :—first, that the colonists were still Englishmen

³ *Letters on Sacramental Test in* 1738.
⁴ To Sir Charles Wigan, July, 1732.
⁵ To Lord Peterborough, April 21st, 1726.

and entitled to English rights ; secondly, that their trade
was deliberately crushed, purely for the benefit of the
English of England ; thirdly, that all valuable preferments
were bestowed upon men born in England, as a matter
of course ; and finally, that in consequence of this, the
upper classes, deprived of all other openings, were forced
to rack-rent their tenants to such a degree that not one
farmer in the kingdom out of a hundred " could afford
shoes or stockings to his children, or to eat flesh or drink
anything better than sour milk and water twice in a year :
so that the whole country, except the Scotch plantation
in the north, is a scene of misery and desolation hardly
to be matched on this side Lapland." A modern reformer
would give the first and chief place to this social misery.
It is characteristic that Swift comes to it as a consequence
from the injustice to his own class :—as, again, that he
appeals to Walpole not on the simple ground that the
people are wretched, but on the ground that they will
be soon unable to pay the tribute to England, which he
reckons at a million a year. But his conclusion might be
accepted by any Irish patriot. Whatever, he says, can
make a country poor and despicable, concurs in the case
of Ireland. The nation is controlled by laws to which
it does not consent ; disowned by its brethren and countrymen ; refused the liberty of trading even in its natural
commodities ; forced to seek for justice many hundred
miles by sea and land ; rendered in a manner incapable of
serving the king and country in any place of honour,
trust, or profit ; whilst the governors have no sympathy
with the governed, except what may occasionally arise
from the sense of justice and philanthropy.

I am not to ask how far Swift was right in his judgments. Every line which he wrote shows that he was

thoroughly sincere and profoundly stirred by his convictions. A remarkable pamphlet, published in 1720, contained his first utterance upon the subject. It is an exhortation to the Irish to use only Irish manufactures. He applies to Ireland the fable of *Arachne and Pallas*. The goddess, indignant at being equalled in spinning, turned her rival into a spider, to spin for ever out of her own bowels in a narrow compass. He always, he says, pitied poor Arachne for so cruel and unjust a sentence, "which, however, is fully executed upon us by England with further additions of rigour and severity ; for the greatest part of our bowels and vitals is extracted, without allowing us the liberty of spinning and weaving them." Swift of course accepts the economic fallacy equally taken for granted by his opponents, and fails to see that England and Ireland injured themselves as well as each other by refusing to interchange their productions. But he utters forcibly his righteous indignation against the contemptuous injustice of the English rulers, in consequence of which the "miserable people" are being reduced "to a worse condition than the peasants in France, or the vassals in Germany and Poland." Slaves, he says, have a natural disposition to be tyrants ; and he himself, when his betters give him a kick, is apt to revenge it with six upon his footman. That is how the landlords treat their tenantry.

The printer of this pamphlet was prosecuted. The chief justice (Whitshed) sent back the jury nine times and kept them eleven hours before they would consent to bring in a "special verdict." The unpopularity of the prosecution became so great that it was at last dropped. Four years afterwards a more violent agitation broke out. A patent had been given to a certain William Wood for supplying Ireland with a copper coinage. Many complaints had been made,

and in September, 1723, addresses were voted by the Irish
Houses of Parliament, declaring that the patent had been
obtained by clandestine and false representations : that it
was mischievous to the country : and that Wood had been
guilty of frauds in his coinage. They were pacified by
vague promises ; but Walpole went on with the scheme on
the strength of a favourable report of a committee of the
Privy Council ; and the excitement was already serious
when (in 1724) Swift published the *Drapier's Letters,*
which give him his chief title to eminence as a patriotic
agitator.

Swift either shared or took advantage of the general
belief that the mysteries of the currency are unfathomable
to the human intelligence. They have to do with that
world of financial magic in which wealth may be made
out of paper, and all ordinary relations of cause and effect
are suspended. There is, however, no real mystery about
the halfpence. The small coins which do not form part
of the legal tender may be considered primarily as
counters. A penny is a penny, so long as twelve are
change for a shilling. It is not in the least necessary for
this purpose that the copper contained in the twelve penny
pieces should be worth or nearly worth a shilling. A
sovereign can never be worth much more than the gold
of which it is made. But at the present day bronze
worth only twopence is coined into twelve penny pieces.[6]
The coined bronze is worth six times as much as the un-
coined. The small coins must have some intrinsic value to
deter forgery, and must be made of good materials to stand
wear and tear. If these conditions be observed, and a proper number be issued, the value of the penny will be no

[6] The ton of bronze, I am informed, is coined into 108,000 pence,
that is 450*l*. The metal is worth about 74*l*.

more affected by the value of the copper than the value of
the banknote by that of the paper on which it is written.
This opinion assumes that the copper coins cannot be
offered or demanded in payment of any but trifling debts.
The halfpence coined by Wood seem to have fulfilled
these conditions, and as copper worth twopence (on the
lowest computation) was coined into ten halfpence, worth
fivepence, their intrinsic value was more than double that
of modern halfpence.

The halfpence, then, were not objectionable upon this
ground. Nay, it would have been wasteful to make them
more valuable. It would have been as foolish to use more
copper for the pence as to make the works of a watch of
gold if brass is equally durable and convenient. But
another consequence is equally clear. The effect of Wood's
patent was that a mass of copper worth about 60,000*l.*,[7]
became worth 100,800*l.* in the shape of halfpenny pieces.
There was therefore a balance of about 40,000*l.* to pay for
the expenses of coinage. It would have been waste to
get rid of this by putting more copper in the coins ; but
if so large a profit arose from the transaction, it would go
to somebody. At the present day it would be brought
into the national treasury. This was not the way in which
business was done in Ireland. Wood was to pay 1000*l.* a
year for fourteen years to the Crown.[8] But 14,000*l.* still
leaves a large margin for profit. What was to become of
it ? According to the admiring biographer of Sir R. Wal-

[7] Simon, in his work on the Irish coinage, makes the profit
60,000*l.*; but he reckons the copper at 1*s.* a lb., whereas from
the Report of the Privy Council it would seem to be properly
1*s.* 6*d.* a lb. Swift and most later writers say 108,000*l.*, but the
right sum is 100,800*l.* 360 tons coined into 2*s.* 6*d.* a lb.

[8] Monck Mason says only 300*l.* a year, but this is the sum mentioned in the Report and by Swift.

pole, the patent had been originally given by Lord Sunderland to the Duchess of Kendal, a lady whom the king
delighted to honour. She already received 3000*l*. a year
in pensions upon the Irish establishment, and she sold
this patent to Wood for 10,000*l*. Enough was still left to
give Wood a handsome profit ; as in transactions of this
kind, every accomplice in a dirty business expects to be
well paid. So handsome, indeed, was the profit that
Wood received ultimately a pension of 3000*l*. for eight
years, 24,000*l*., that is, in consideration of abandoning the
patent. It was right and proper that a profit should be
made on the transaction, but shameful that it should be
divided between the king's mistress and William Wood,
and that the bargain should be struck without con-
sulting the Irish representatives, and maintained in spite
of their protests. The Duchess of Kendal was to be
allowed to take a share of the wretched halfpence in the
pocket of every Irish beggar. A more disgraceful transaction could hardly be imagined, or one more calculated to
justify Swift's view of the selfishness and corruption of
the English rulers.

Swift saw his chance, and went to work in characteristic
fashion, with unscrupulous audacity of statement, guided
by the keenest strategical instinct. He struck at the heart
as vigorously as he had done in the *Examiner*, but with
resentment sharpened by ten years of exile. It was not
safe to speak of the Duchess of Kendal's share in the
transaction, though the story, as poor Archdeacon Coxe
pathetically declares, was industriously propagated. But
the case against Wood was all the stronger. Is he so
wicked, asks Swift, as to suppose that a nation is to be
ruined that he may gain three or fourscore thousand
pounds ? Hampden went to prison, he says, rather than

pay a few shillings wrongfully ; I, says Swift, would
rather be hanged than have all my "property taxed at
seventeen shillings in the pound at the arbitrary will and
pleasure of the venerable Mr. Wood." A simple constitutional precedent might rouse a Hampden ; but to stir a popular agitation, it is as well to show that the evil actually
inflicted is gigantic, independently of possible results.   It
requires, indeed, some audacity to prove that debasement
of the copper currency can amount to a tax of seventeen
shillings in the pound on all property.   Here, however,
Swift might simply throw the reins upon the neck of his
fancy.   Anybody may make any inferences he pleases in
the mysterious regions of currency ; and no inferences, it
seems, were too audacious for his hearers, though we are left
to doubt how far Swift's wrath had generated delusions in
his own mind, and how far he perceived that other minds
were ready to be deluded.   He revels in prophesying the
most extravagant consequences.   The country will be undone ; the tenants will not be able to pay their rents ; "the
farmers must rob, or beg, or leave the country ; the shop-
keepers in this and every other town must break or starve ;
the squire will hoard up all his good money to send to
England and keep some poor tailor or weaver in his
house, who will be glad to get bread at any rate." [9]   Concrete facts are given to help the imagination.   Squire
Conolly must have 250 horses to bring his half-yearly
rents to town ; and the poor man will have to pay thirty-
six of Wood's halfpence to get a quart of twopenny ale.

How is this proved ?   One argument is a sufficient specimen.   Nobody, according to the patent, was to be forced
to take Wood's halfpence ; nor could any one be obliged

[9] Letter I.

to receive more than fivepence halfpenny in any one payment. This, of course, meant that the halfpence could
only be used as change, and a man must pay his debts
in silver or gold whenever it was possible to use a sixpence.
It upsets Swift's statement about Squire Connolly's rents.
But Swift is equal to the emergency. The rule means,
he says, that every man must take fivepence halfpenny in
every payment, *if it be offered;* which, on the next page,
becomes simply in every payment ; therefore making an
easy assumption or two, he reckons that you will receive
160*l.* a year in these halfpence ; and therefore (by other
assumptions) lose 140*l.* a year.[1] It might have occurred
to Swift, one would think, that both parties to the transaction could not possibly be losers. But he calmly
assumes that the man who pays will lose in proportion to
the increased number of coins; and the man who receives,
in proportion to the depreciated value of each coin. He
does not see, or think it worth notice, that the two losses
obviously counterbalance each other ; and he has an easy
road to prophesying absolute ruin for everybody. It
would be almost as great a compliment to call this
sophistry, as to dignify with the name of satire a round
assertion that an honest man is a cheat or a rogue.

The real grievance, however, shows through the sham
argument. "It is no loss of honour," thought Swift, "to
submit to the lion ; but who, with the figure of a man,
can think with patience of being devoured alive by a
rat ? " Why should Wood have this profit (even if more
reasonably estimated) in defiance of the wishes of the
nation ? It is, says Swift, because he is an Englishman
and has great friends. He proposes to meet the attempt

[1] Letter II.

by a general agreement not to take the halfpence. Briefly, the halfpence were to be "Boycotted."

Before this second letter was written the English ministers had become alarmed. A Report of the Privy Council (July 24, 1724) defended the patent, but ended by recommending that the amount to be coined should be reduced to 40,000*l*. Carteret was sent out as Lord Lieutenant to get this compromise accepted. Swift replied by a third letter, arguing the question of the patent, which he can "never suppose," or in other words, which everybody knew, to have been granted as a "job for the interest of some particular person." He vigorously asserts that the patent can never make it obligatory to accept the halfpence, and tells a story much to the purpose from old Leicester experience. The justices had reduced the price of ale to three-halfpence a quart. One of them therefore requested that they would make another order to appoint who should drink it, "for by God," said he, "I will not."

The argument thus naturally led to a further and more important question. The discussion as to the patent brought forward the question of right. Wood and his friends, according to Swift, had begun to declare that the resistance meant Jacobitism and rebellion ; they asserted that the Irish were ready to shake off their dependence upon the crown of England. Swift took up the challenge and answered resolutely and eloquently. He took up the broadest ground. Ireland, he declared, depended upon England in no other sense than that in which England depended upon Ireland. Whoever thinks otherwise, he said, "I, M. B. despair, desire to be excepted ; for I declare, next under God, I depend only on the king my sovereign, and the laws of my own country. I am so

far," he added, "from depending upon the people of
England, that if they should rebel, I would take arms
and lose every drop of my blood, to hinder the Pretender
from being king of Ireland."

It had been reported that somebody (Walpole presumably) had sworn to thrust the halfpence down the throats
of the Irish. The remedy, replied Swift, is totally in your
own hands, " and therefore I have digressed a litttle . . . .
to let you see that by the laws of God, of Nature, of
Nations, and of your own country, you are and ought to
be as free a people as your brethren in England." As
Swift had already said in the third letter, no one could
believe that any English patent would stand half an hour
after an address from the English houses of Parliament
such as that which had been passed against Wood's by
the Irish Parliament. Whatever constitutional doubts
might be raised, it was therefore come to be the plain
question whether or not the English ministers should
simply override the wishes of the Irish nation.

Carteret, upon landing, began by trying to suppress
his adversary. A reward of 300*l.* was offered for the
discovery of the author of the fourth letter. A prosecution was ordered against the printer. Swift went to the
levée of the Lord Lieutenant, and reproached him bitterly
for his severity against a poor tradesman who had
published papers for the good of his country. Carteret
answered in a happy quotation from Virgil, a feat which
always seems to have brought consolation to the statesman
of that day.

> Res dura et regni novitas me talia cogunt
> Moliri.

Another story is more characteristic. Swift's butler

had acted as his amanuensis, and absented himself one
night whilst the proclamation was running. Swift
thought that the butler was either treacherous or presuming upon his knowledge of the secret. As soon as the
man returned he ordered him to strip off his livery and
begone. " I am in your power," he said, " and for that very
reason I will not stand your insolence." The poor butler
departed, but preserved his fidelity; and Swift, when
the tempest had blown over, rewarded him by appointing
him verger in the cathedral. The grand jury threw out
the bill against the printer in spite of all Whitshed's
efforts ; they were discharged ; and the next grand jury
presented Wood's halfpence as a nuisance. Carteret
gave way, the patent was surrendered, and Swift might
congratulate himself upon a complete victory.

The conclusion is in one respect rather absurd. The
Irish succeeded in rejecting a real benefit at the cost of
paying Wood the profit which he would have made, had
he been allowed to confer it. Another point must be
admitted. Swift's audacious misstatements were successful for the time in rousing the spirit of the people. They
have led, however, to a very erroneous estimate of the
whole case. English statesmen and historians [2] have
found it so easy to expose his errors that they have
thought his whole case absurd. The grievance was not
what it was represented, therefore it is argued that there
was no grievance. The very essence of the case was that
the Irish people were to be plundered by the German
mistress; and such plunder was possible because the
English people, as Swift says, never thought of Ireland

[2] See for example Lord Stanhope's account. For the other view
see Mr. Lecky's *History of the Eighteenth Century,* and Mr. Froude's
English in Ireland.

except when there was nothing else to be talked of in the coffee-houses.[3] Owing to the conditions of the controversy, this grievance only came out gradually, and could never be fully stated. Swift could never do more than hint at the transaction. His letters (including three which appeared after the last mentioned, enforcing the same case) have often been cited as models of eloquence, and compared to Demosthenes. We must make some deduction from this, as in the case of his former political pamphlets. The intensity of his absorption in the immediate end, deprives them of some literary merits ; and we, to whom the sophistries are palpable enough, are apt to resent them. Anybody can be effective in a way, if he chooses to lie boldly. Yet, in another sense, it is hard to over-praise the letters. They have in a high degree the peculiar stamp of Swift's genius ; the vein of the most nervous commonsense and pithy assertion with an undercurrent of intense passion, the more impressive because it is never allowed to exhale in mere rhetoric.

Swift's success, the dauntless front which he had shown to the oppressor, made him the idol of his countrymen. A drapier's club was formed in his honour, which collected the letters and drank toasts and sang songs to celebrate their hero. In a sad letter to Pope, in 1737, he complains that none of his equals care for him ; but adds that as he walks the streets he has " a thousand hats and blessings upon old scores which those we call the gentry have forgot." The people received him as their champion. When he returned from England in 1726, bells were rung, bonfires lighted and a guard of honour escorted him to the deanery. Towns voted him

[3] Letter IV.

their freedom and received him like a prince. When
Walpole spoke of arresting him, a prudent friend told
the minister that the messenger would require a guard of
10,000 soldiers. Corporations asked his advice in elections, and the weavers appealed to him on questions about
their trade. In one of his satires,[4] Swift had attacked a
certain Serjeant Bettesworth—

> Thus at the bar the booby Bettesworth
> Though half-a-crown o'erpays his sweat's worth.

Bettesworth called upon him with, as Swift reports, a
knife in his pocket, and complained in such terms as
to imply some intention of personal violence. The
neighbours instantly sent a deputation to the dean,
proposing to take vengeance upon Bettesworth, and
though he induced them to disperse peaceably, they formed
a guard to watch the house; and Bettesworth complained
that his attack upon the dean had lowered his professional
income by 1200*l.* a year. A quaint example of his popu-
larity is given by Sheridan. A great crowd had collected
to see an eclipse. Swift thereupon sent out the bellman
to give notice that the eclipse had been postponed by
the dean's orders; and the crowd dispersed.

Influence with the people, however, could not bring
Swift back to power. At one time there seemed to be
a gleam of hope. Swift visited England twice in 1726
and 1727. He paid long visits to his old friend Pope,
and again met Bolingbroke, now returned from exile,
and trying to make a place in English politics. Peterborough introduced the dean to Walpole, to whom Swift
detailed his views upon Irish politics. Walpole was
the last man to set about a great reform from mere con-

[4] "On the words Brother Protestants, &c."

M

siderations of justice and philanthropy, and was not likely
to trust a confidant of Bolingbroke. He was civil but
indifferent. Swift, however, was introduced by his
friends to Mrs. Howard, the mistress of the Prince of
Wales, soon to become George II. The princess, afterwards Queen Caroline, ordered Swift to come and see
her, and he complied, as he says, after nine commands.
He told her that she had lately seen a wild boy from
Germany, and now he supposed she wanted to see a
wild dean from Ireland. Some civilities passed; Swift
offered some plaids of Irish manufacture, and the princess
promised some medals in return. When, in the next
year, George I. died, the Opposition hoped great things
from the change. Pulteney had tried to get Swift's
powerful help for the *Craftsman*, the Opposition organ;
and the Opposition hoped to upset Walpole. Swift, who
had thought of going to France for his health, asked
Mrs. Howard's advice. She recommended him to stay;
and he took the recommendation as amounting to a
promise of support. He had some hopes of obtaining
English preferment in exchange for his deanery in what
he calls (in the date to one of his letters [5]) "wretched
Dublin in miserable Ireland." It soon appeared, however, that the mistress was powerless; and that Walpole
was to be as firm as ever in his seat. Swift returned to
Ireland, never again to leave it: to lose soon afterwards
his beloved Stella, and nurse an additional grudge against
courts and favourites.

The bitterness with which he resented Mrs. Howard's
supposed faithlessness is painfully illustrative in truth of
the morbid state of mind which was growing upon him.

[5] To Lord Stafford, Nov. 26, 1725.

"You think," he says to Bolingbroke in 1729, " as I ought
to think, that it is time for me to have done with the
world ; and so I would, if I could get into a better
before I was called into the best, and not die here in
a rage, like a poisoned rat in a hole." That terrible
phrase expresses but too vividly the state of mind which
was now becoming familiar to him. Separated by death
and absence from his best friends, and tormented by increasing illness, he looked out upon a state of things
in which he could see no ground for hope. The resistance to Wood's halfpence had staved off immediate ruin ;
but had not cured the fundamental evil. Some tracts
upon Irish affairs, written after the Drapier's Letters,
sufficiently indicate his despairing vein. " I am," he says
in 1737, when proposing some remedy for the swarms of
beggars in Dublin, " a desponder by nature," and he has
found out that the people will never stir themselves to
remove a single grievance. His old prejudices were as
keen as ever, and could dictate personal outbursts. He
attacked the bishops bitterly for offering certain measures
which in his view sacrificed the permanent interests of
the Church to that of the actual occupants. He showed
his own sincerity by refusing to take fines for leases
which would have benefited himself at the expense of
his successors. With equal earnestness he still clung to
the Test Acts, and assailed the Protestant dissenters with
all his old bitterness, and ridiculed their claims to brother-
hood with Churchmen. To the end he was a Churchman
before everything. One of the last of his poetical performances was prompted by the sanction given by the
Irish Parliament to an opposition to certain " titles of
ejectment." He had defended the right of the Irish
Parliament against English rulers ; but when it attacked

the interests of his Church his fury showed itself in the
most savage satire that he ever wrote, the *Legion Club*.
It is an explosion of wrath tinged with madness.

> Could I from the building's top
> Hear the rattling thunder drop,
> While the devil upon the roof
> (If the devil be thunder-proof)
> Should with poker fiery red
> Crack the stones and melt the lead,
> Drive them down on every skull
> When the den of thieves is full;
> Quite destroy the harpies' nest,
> How might this our isle be blest!

What follows fully keeps up to this level. Swift flings
filth like a maniac, plunges into ferocious personalities, and
ends fitly with the execration,—

> May their God, the devil, confound them.

He was seized with one of his fits whilst writing the poem
and was never afterwards capable of sustained composition.
   Some further pamphlets—especially one on the State
of Ireland—repeat and enforce his views.   One of them
requires special mention.   The *Modest Proposal* (written
in 1729) *for Preventing the Children of Poor People in
Ireland from being a Burden to their Parents or Country*—
the proposal being that they should be turned into articles
of food—gives the very essence of Swift's feeling, and
is one of the most tremendous pieces of satire in existence.
It shows the quality already noticed.   Swift is burning
with a passion, the glow of which makes other passions
look cold, as it is said that some bright lights cause other
illuminating objects to cast a shadow.   Yet his face is
absolutely grave, and he details his plan as calmly as a

modern projector suggesting the importation of Australian
meat. The superficial coolness may be revolting to tender-
hearted people, and has indeed led to condemnation of
the supposed ferocity of the author almost as surprising as
the criticisms which can see in it nothing but an exquisite
piece of humour. It is, in truth, fearful to read even now.
Yet we can forgive and even sympathize when we take it
for what it really is—the most complete expression of
burning indignation against intolerable wrongs. It utters,
indeed, a serious conviction. "I confess myself," says
Swift in a remarkable paper,[6] "to be touched with a very
sensible pleasure when I hear of a mortality in any
country parish or village, where the wretches are forced
to pay for a filthy cabin and two ridges of potatoes
treble the worth; brought up to steal and beg for want
of work; to whom death would be the best thing to be
wished for, on account both of themselves and the public."
He remarks in the same place on the lamentable contradiction presented in Ireland to the maxim that the "people
are the riches of a nation," and the *Modest Proposal* is the
fullest comment on this melancholy reflection. After
many visionary proposals, he has at last hit upon the plan,
which has at least the advantage that by adopting it "we
can incur no danger of disobliging England. For this kind
of commodity will not bear exportation, the flesh being of
too tender a consistence to admit a long continuance in
salt, although perhaps I could name a country which
would be glad to eat up a whole nation without it."

Swift once asked Delany[7] whether the "corruptions
and villanies of men in power did not eat his flesh and
exhaust his spirits?" "No," said Delany. "Why, how

---

[6] *Maxims Controuled in Ireland.*   [7] *Delany*, p. 148.

can you help it?" said Swift. "Because," replied
Delany, "I am commanded to the contrary—*fret not thy-
self because of the ungodly.*" That, like other wise maxims,
is capable of an ambiguous application. As Delany took it,
Swift might perhaps have replied that it was a very comfortable maxim—for the ungodly. His own application of
Scripture is different. It tells us, he says, in his proposal
for using Irish manufactures, that "oppression makes a
wise man mad." If, therefore, some men are not mad, it
must be because they are not wise. In truth, it is characteristic of Swift that he could never learn the great lesson
of submission even to the inevitable. He could not, like
an easy-going Delany, submit to oppression which might
possibly be resisted with success; but as little could he
submit when all resistance was hopeless. His rage, which
could find no better outlet, burnt inwardly and drove him
mad. It is very interesting to compare Swift's wrathful
denunciations with Berkeley's treatment of the same before
in the *Querist* (1735-7). Berkeley is full of luminous
suggestions upon economical questions which are entirely
beyond Swift's mark. He is in a region quite above the
sophistries of the *Drapier's Letters.* He sees equally the
terrible grievance that no people in the world is so beggarly,
wretched, and destitute as the common Irish. But he thinks
all complaints against the English rule useless and therefore
foolish. If the English restrain our trade ill-advisedly, is it
not, he asks, plainly our interest to accommodate ourselves
to them (No. 136). Have we not the advantage of English
protection without sharing English responsibilities? He
asks, "whether England doth not really love us and wish
well to us as bone of her bone and flesh of her flesh? and
whether it be not our part to cultivate this love and affection all manner of ways?" (Nos. 322, 323.) One can

fancy how Swift must have received this characteristic suggestion of the admirable Berkeley, who could not bring himself to think ill of any one. Berkeley's main contention is no doubt sound in itself, namely, that the welfare of the country really depended on the industry and economy of its inhabitants, and that such qualities would have made the Irish comfortable in spite of all English restrictions and Government abuses. But, then, Swift might well have answered that such general maxims are idle. It is all very well for divines to tell people to become good and to find out that then they will be happy. But how are they to be made good? Are the Irish intrinsically worse than other men, or is their laziness and restlessness due to special and removable circumstances? In the latter case is there not more real value in attacking tangible evils than in propounding general maxims and calling upon all men to submit to oppression, and even to believe in the oppressor's good-will in the name of Christian charity? To answer those questions would be to plunge into interminable and hopeless controversies. Meanwhile Swift's fierce indignation against English oppression might almost as well have been directed against a law of nature for any immediate result. Whether the rousing of the national spirit was any benefit is a question which I must leave to others. In any case, the work, however darkened by personal feeling or love of class-privilege, expressed as hearty a hatred of oppression as ever animated a human being.

CHAPTER VIII.

THE winter of 1713-14 passed by Swift in England was
full of anxiety and vexation. He found time, however,
to join in a remarkable literary association. The so-called
Scriblerus Club does not appear, indeed, to have had any
definite organization. The rising young wits, Pope and
Gay, both of them born in 1688, were already becoming
famous, and were taken up by Swift, still in the zenith of
his political power. Parnell, a few years their senior, had
been introduced by Swift to Oxford as a convert from
Whiggism. All three became intimate with Swift and
Arbuthnot, the most learned and amiable of the whole
circle of Swift's friends. Swift declared him to have
every quality that could make a man amiable and useful
with but one defect—he had "a sort of slouch in his
walk ;" he was loved and respected by every one, and was
one of the most distinguished of the Brothers. Swift and
Arbuthnot and their three juniors discussed literary plans
in the midst of the growing political excitement. Even
Oxford used, as Pope tells us, to amuse himself during
the very crisis of his fate by scribbling verses and talking
nonsense with the members of this informal Club, and
some doggerel lines exchanged with him remain as a specimen—a poor one it is to be hoped—of their intercourse.

The familiarity thus begun continued through the life of the members. Swift can have seen very little of Pope. He hardly made his acquaintance till the latter part of 1713; they parted in the summer of 1714; and never met again except in Swift's two visits to England in 1726-27. Yet their correspondence shows an affection which was no doubt heightened by the consciousness of each that the friendship of his most famous contemporary author was creditable; but which, upon Swift's side at least, was thoroughly sincere and cordial, and strengthened with advancing years.

The final cause of the Club was supposed to be the composition of a joint-stock satire. We learn from an interesting letter [1] that Pope formed the original design; though Swift thought that Arbuthnot was the only one capable of carrying it out. The scheme was to write the memoirs of an imaginary pedant, who had dabbled with equal wrong-headedness in all kinds of knowledge; and thus recalls Swift's early performances—the *Battle of the Books* and the *Tale of a Tub*. Arbuthnot begs Swift to work upon it during his melancholy retirement at Letcombe. Swift had other things to occupy his mind; and upon the dispersion of the party the Club fell into abeyance. Fragments of the original plan were carried out by Pope and Arbuthnot, and form part of the *Miscellanies*, to which Swift contributed a number of poetical scraps, published under Pope's direction in 1726-27. It seems probable that *Gulliver* originated in Swift's mind in the course of his meditations upon Scriblerus. The composition of *Gulliver* was one of the occupations by which he amused himself after recovering from the great shock of

[1] It is in the Forster library, and, I believe, unpublished, in answer to Arbuthnot's letter mentioned in the text.

his " exile." He worked, as he seems always to have done, slowly and intermittently. Part of Brobdingnag at least, as we learn from a letter of Vanessa's, was in existence by 1722. Swift brought the whole manuscript to England in 1726, and it was published anonymously in the following winter. The success was instantaneous and overwhelming. " I will make over all my profits " (in a work then being published) "to you," writes Arbuthnot, "for the property of *Gulliver's Travels*, which, I believe, will have as great a run as John Bunyan." The anticipation was amply fulfilled. *Gulliver's Travels* is one of the very few books some knowledge of which may be fairly assumed in any one who reads anything. Yet something must be said of the secret of the astonishing success of this unique performance.

One remark is obvious. *Gulliver's Travels* (omitting certain passages) is almost the most delightful children's book ever written. Yet it has been equally valued as an unrivalled satire. Old Sarah, Duchess of Marlborough, was "in raptures with it," says Gay, "and can dream of nothing else." She forgives his bitter attacks upon her party in consideration of his assault upon human nature. He gives, she declares, "the most accurate" (that is, of course, the most scornful) "account of kings, ministers, bishops, and courts of justice, that is possible to be writ." Another curious testimony may be noticed. Godwin, when tracing all evils to the baneful effects of government, declares that the author of *Gulliver* showed a " more profound insight into the true principles of political justice than any preceding or contemporary author." The playful form was unfortunate, thinks this grave philosopher, as blinding mankind to the " inestimable wisdom " of the work. This double triumph is remarkable. We may not share the opinions of the cynics of the day, or of the revolutionists of a later generation ; but it is strange that they should be fascinated by a work which is studied with delight, without the faintest suspicion of any ulterior meaning, by the infantile mind.

The charm of Gulliver for the young depends upon an obvious quality, which is indicated in Swift's report of the criticism by an Irish bishop, who said that "the book was full of improbable lies, and for his part he hardly believed a word of it." There is something pleasant in the intense gravity of the narrative, which recalls and may have been partly suggested by *Robinson Crusoe*, though it came naturally to Swift. I have already spoken of his delight in mystification, and the detailed realization of pure fiction seems to have been delightful in itself. The Partridge pamphlets and its various practical jokes are illustrations of a tendency which fell in with the spirit of the time, and of which *Gulliver* may be regarded as the highest manifestation. Swift's peculiarity is in the curious sobriety of fancy, which leads him to keep in his most daring flights upon the confines of the possible. In the imaginary travels of Lucian and Rabelais, to which *Gulliver* is generally compared, we frankly take leave of the real world altogether. We are treated with arbitrary and monstrous combinations which may be amusing, but which do not challenge even a semblance of belief. In *Gulliver* this is so little the case that it can hardly be said in strictness that the fundamental assumptions are even impossible. Why should there not be creatures in human form with whom as in Lilliput, one of our inches represents a foot, or, as in Brobdingnag, one of our feet represents an inch ? The assumption is so modest that we are presented—it may be said—with a definite and

soluble problem. We have not, as in other fictitious
worlds, to deal with a state of things in which the imagination is bewildered, but with one in which it is agreeably
stimulated. We have certainly to consider an extreme and
exceptional case ; but one to which all the ordinary laws
of human nature are still strictly applicable. In Voltaire's
trifle, *Micromegas*, we are presented to beings eight
leagues in height and endowed with seventy-two senses.
For Voltaire's purpose the stupendous exaggeration is
necessary ; for he wishes to insist upon the minuteness of
human capacities. But the assumption of course dis-
qualifies us from taking any intelligent interest in a region
where no precedent is available for our guidance. We
are in the air ; anything and everything is possible. But
Swift modestly varies only one element in the problem.
Imagine giants and dwarfs as tall as a house or as low as
a footstool, and let us see what comes of it. That is a
plain, almost a mathematical problem ; and we can therefore judge his success, and receive pleasure from the
ingenuity and verisimilitude of his creations.

" When you have once thought of big men and little
men," said Johnson, perversely enough, " it is easy to do
the rest." The first step might perhaps seem in this case
to be the easiest ; yet nobody ever thought of it before
Swift ; and nobody has ever had similar good fortune
since. There is no other fictitious world the denizens of
which have become so real for us, and which has supplied
so many images familiar to every educated mind. But
the apparent ease is due to the extreme consistency and
sound judgment of Swift's realization. The conclusions
follow so inevitably from the primary data that when
they are once drawn we agree that they could not have
been otherwise ; and infer, rashly, that anybody else could

have drawn them.   It is as easy as lying ; but everybody
who has seriously tried the experiment knows that
even lying is by no means so easy as it appears at
first sight.   In fact, Swift's success is something unique.
The charming plausibility of every incident, throughout
the two first parts, commends itself to children, who enjoy
definite concrete images, and are fascinated by a world
which is at once full of marvels, surpassing Jack the Giant
Killer and the wonders seen by Sinbad, and yet as obviously and undeniably true as the adventures of Robinson
Crusoe himself.   Nobody who has read the book can
ever forget it ; and we may add that besides the child-
like pleasure which arises from a distinct realization of a
strange world of fancy, the two first books are sufficiently
good-humoured.   Swift seems to be amused as well as amus.
ing.   They were probably written during the least intolerable
part of his exile.   The period of composition includes the
years of the Vanessa tragedy and of the war of Wood's
halfpence ;   it was finished when Stella's illness was
becoming constantly more threatening, and published
little more than a year before her death.   The last books
show Swift's most savage temper ; but we may hope that
in spite of disease, disappointments, and a growing alienation from mankind, Swift could still enjoy an occasional
piece of spontaneous, unadulterated fun.   He could still
forget his cares, and throw the reins on the neck of his
fancy.   At times there is a certain charm even in the
characters.   Every one has a liking for the giant maid of
all work, Glumdalelitch, whose affection for her plaything
is a quaint inversion of the ordinary relations between
Swift and his feminine adorers.   The grave, stern, irascible
man can relax after a sort, though his strange idiosyncrasy
comes out as distinctly in his relaxation as in his passions.

I will not dwell upon this aspect of *Gulliver*, which is
obvious to every one. There is another question which
we are forced to ask, and which is not very easy to answer.
What does *Gulliver* mean? It is clearly a satire—but
who and what are its objects? Swift states his own
view very unequivocally. "I heartily hate and detest
that animal called man," he says,[2] "although I heartily
love John, Peter, Thomas, and so forth." He declares that
man is not an *animal rationale*, but only *rationis capax*:
and he then adds, "Upon this great foundation of
misanthropy . . . . the whole building of my travels is
erected." "If the world had but a dozen Arbuthnots in
it," he says in the same letter, "I would burn my
travels." He indulges in a similar reflection to Sheridan.[3]
"Expect no more from man," he says, "than such an
animal is capable of, and you will every day find my
description of Yahoos more resembling. You should
think and deal with every man as a villain, without
calling him so, or flying from him or valuing him less.
This is an old true lesson." In spite of these avowals, of
a kind which, in Swift, must not be taken too literally,
we find it rather hard to admit that the essence of
Gulliver can be an expression of this doctrine. · The tone
becomes morose and sombre, and even ferocious; but it
has been disputed whether in any case it can be regarded
simply as an utterance of misanthropy.

Gulliver's Travels belongs to a literary genus full of
grotesque and anomalous forms. Its form is derived from
some of the imaginary travels of which Lucian's *True
History*—itself a burlesque of some early travellers' tales—
is the first example. But it has an affinity also to such

2 Letter to Pope, Sept. 29th, 1725.
3 Letter to Sheridan, Sept. 11th, 1725.

books as Bacon's *Atlantis*, and More's *Utopia ;* and, again,
to later philosophical romances like *Candide* and *Ras-
selas ;* and not least, perhaps, to the ancient fables, such as
Reynard the Fox, to which Swift refers in the *Tale of a
Tub.* It may be compared, again, to the *Pilgrim's Progress*, and the whole family of allegories.   The full-blown
allegory resembles the game of chess said to have been
played by some ancient monarch, in which the pieces
were replaced by real human beings.   The movements of
the actors were not determined by the passions proper to
their character, but by the external set of rules imposed
upon them by the game.   The allegory is a kind of
picture-writing, popular, like picture-writing at a certain
stage of development, but wearisome at more cultivated
periods, when we prefer to have abstract theories conveyed in abstract language, and limit the artist to the
intrinsic meanings of the images in which he deals.   The
whole class of more or less allegorical writing has thus
the peculiarity that something more is meant than meets
the ear.   Part of its meaning depends upon a tacit convention in virtue of which a beautiful woman, for
example, is not simply a beautiful woman, but also a
representative of Justice and Charity.   And as any such
convention is more or less arbitrary, we are often in per-
plexity to interpret the author's meaning, and also to
judge of the propriety of the symbols.   The allegorical
intention, again, may be more or less present : and such a
book as Gulliver must be regarded as lying somewhere
between the allegory and the direct revelation of truth,
which is more or less implied in the work of every
genuine artist.   Its true purpose has thus rather puzzled
critics.   Hazlitt [4] urges, for example, with his usual

4 *Lectures on the English Poets.*

brilliancy, that Swift's purpose was to "strip empty pride
and grandeur of the imposing air which external circumstances throw around them." Swift accordingly varies
the scale, so as to show the insignificance or the grossness
of our self-love. He does this with "mathematical precision;" he tries an experiment upon human nature; and
with the result that "nothing solid, nothing valuable is
left in his system but wisdom and virtue." So Gulliver's
carrying off the fleet of Blefuscu is "a mortifying
stroke, aimed at national glory." "After that, we have
only to consider which of the contending parties was in
the right."

Hazlitt naturally can see nothing misanthropical or
innocent in such a conclusion. The mask of imposture is
torn off the world, and only imposture can complain.
This view, which has no doubt its truth, suggests some
obvious doubts. We are not invited, as a matter of fact,
to attend to the question of right and wrong, as between
Lilliput and Blefuscu. The real sentiment in Swift is
that a war between these miserable pygmies is, in itself,
contemptible; and therefore, as he infers, war between
men six feet high is equally contemptible. The truth is
that, although Swift's solution of the problem may be
called mathematically precise, the precision does not
extend to the supposed argument. If we insist upon
treating the question as one of strict logic, the only conclusion which could be drawn from Gulliver is the very
safe one that the interest of the human drama does not
depend upon the size of the actors. A pygmy or a giant
endowed with all our functions and thoughts would be
exactly as interesting as a being of the normal stature.
It does not require a journey to imaginary regions to
teach us so much. And if we say that Swift has shown

us in his pictures the real essence of human life, we only say for him what might be said with equal force of Shakspeare or Balzac, or any great artist. The bare proof that the essence is not dependent upon the external condition of size is superfluous and irrelevant; and we must admit that Swift's method is childish, or that it does not adhere to this strict logical canon.

Hazlitt, however, comes nearer the truth, as I think, when he says that Swift takes a view of human nature such as might be taken by a being of a higher sphere. That, at least, is his purpose; only, as I think, he pursues it by a neglect of "scientific reasoning." The use of the machinery is simply to bring us into a congenial frame of mind. He strikes the key-note of contempt by his imagery of dwarfs and giants. We despise the petty quarrels of beings six inches high; and therefore we are prepared to despise the wars carried on by a Marlborough and a Eugene. We transfer the contempt based upon mere size, to the motives, which are the same in big men and little. The argument, if argument there be, is a fallacy; but it is equally efficacious for the feelings. You see the pettiness and cruelty of the Lilliputians, who want to conquer an empire defended by toy-ships; and you are tacitly invited to consider whether the bigness of French men-of-war makes an attack upon them more respectable. The force of the satire depends ultimately upon the vigour with which Swift has described the real passions of human beings, big or little. He really means to express a bitter contempt for statesmen and warriors, and seduces us to his side, for the moment, by asking us to look at a diminutive representation of the same beings. The quarrels which depend upon the difference between the high-boots and the low-heeled shoes; or upon breaking eggs

N

at the big or little end ; the party intrigues which are settled
by cutting capers on the tight-rope, are meant, of course,
in ridicule of political and religious parties ; and its force
depends upon our previous conviction that the party-
quarrels between our fellows are, in fact, equally contemptible.   Swift's satire is congenial to the mental
attitude of all who have persuaded themselves that men
are, in fact, a set of contemptible fools and knaves, in
whose quarrels and mutual slaughterings the wise and
good could not persuade themselves to take a serious
interest.   He " proves " nothing, mathematically or otherwise.   If you do not share his sentiments, there is nothing
in the mere alteration of the scale to convince you
that they are right ; you may say, with Hazlitt, that
heroism is as admirable in a Lilliputian as in a Brobding-
nagian, and believe that war calls forth patriotism, and
often advances civilization.   What Swift has really
done is to provide for the man who despises his species
a number of exceedingly effective symbols for the utterance of his contempt.   A child is simply amused with
Bigendians and Littleendians ; a philosopher thinks that
the questions really at the bottom of church quarrels are
in reality of more serious import : but the cynic who has
learnt to disbelieve in the nobility or wisdom of the
great mass of his species finds a most convenient meta-
phor for expressing his disbelief.   In this way *Gulliver's
Travels* contains a whole gallery of caricatures thoroughly
congenial to the despisers of humanity.

In Brobdingnag Swift is generally said to be looking,
as Scott expresses it, through the other end of the tele-
scope.   He wishes to show the grossness of men's passions,
as before he has shown their pettiness.   Some of the incidents are devised in this sense ; but we may notice that

in Brobdingnag he recurs to the Lilliput view. He gives
such an application to his fable as may be convenient,
without bothering himself as to logical consistency. He
points out indeed the disgusting appearances which would
be presented by a magnified human body ; but the King
of Brobdingnag looks down upon Gulliver, just as Gulliver
looked down upon the Lilliputians. The monarch sums
up his view emphatically enough by saying, after listening
to Gulliver's version of modern history, that "the bulk of
your natives appear to me to be the most pernicious race
of little odious vermin that Nature ever suffered to crawl
upon the face of the earth." In Lilliput and Brobdingnag, however, the satire scarcely goes beyond pardonable
limits.   The details are often simply amusing, such as
Gulliver's fear when he gets home, of trampling upon the
pygmies whom he sees around him. And even the severest
satire may be taken without offence by every one who
believes that petty motives, folly and selfishness, play a
large enough part in human life to justify some indignant
exaggerations.   It is in the later parts that the ferocity
of the man utters itself more fully.   The ridicule of the
inventors in the third book is, as Arbuthnot said at
once, the least successful part of the whole ; not only because Swift was getting beyond his knowledge, and beyond
the range of his strongest antipathies, but also because
there is no longer the ingenious plausibility of the earlier
books.   The voyage to the Houyhnhnms, which forms
the best part, is more powerful, but more painful and
repulsive.

A word must here be said of the most unpleasant part
of Swift's character. A morbid interest in the physically
disgusting is shown in several of his writings.   Some
minor pieces, which ought to have been burnt, simply

make the gorge rise. Mrs. Pilkington tells us, and we can for once believe her, that one " poem " actually made her mother sick. It is idle to excuse this on the ground of contemporary freedom of speech. His contemporaries were heartily disgusted. Indeed, though it is true that they revealed certain propensities more openly, I see no reason to think that such propensities were really stronger in them than in their descendants. The objection to Swift is not that he spoke plainly, but that he brooded over filth unnecessarily. No parallel can be found for his tendency even in writers, for example, like Smollett and Fielding, who can be coarse enough when they please, but whose freedom of speech reveals none of Swift's morbid tendency. His indulgence in revolting images is to some extent an indication of a diseased condition of his mind, perhaps of actual mental decay. Delany says that it grew upon him in his later years, and, very gratuitously, attributes it to Pope's influence. The peculiarity is the more remarkable, because Swift was a man of the most scrupulous personal cleanliness. He was always enforcing this virtue with special emphasis. He was rigorously observant of decency in ordinary conversation. Delany once saw him " fall into a furious resentment " with Stella for " a very small failure of delicacy." So far from being habitually coarse, he pushed fastidiousness to the verge of prudery. It is one of the superficial paradoxes of Swift's character that this very shrinking from filth became perverted into an apparently opposite tendency. In truth, his intense repugnance to certain images led him to use them as the only adequate expression of his savage contempt. Instances might be given in some early satires, and in the attack upon dissenters in the *Tale of a Tub*. His intensity of loathing

leads him to besmear his antagonists with filth.   He becomes disgusting in the effort to express his disgust.   As
his misanthropy deepened, he applied the same method
to mankind at large.   He tears aside the veil of decency
to show the bestial elements of human nature ; and his
characteristic irony makes him preserve an apparent calm-
ness during the revolting exhibition.   His state of mind
is strictly analogous to that of some religious ascetics, who
stimulate their contempt for the flesh by fixing their gaze
upon decaying bodies.   They seek to check the love of
beauty by showing us beauty in the grave.   The cynic in
Mr. Tennyson's poem tells us that every face, however
full—

> Padded round with flesh and blood,
> Is but moulded on a skull.

Swift—a practised self-tormentor, though not in the
ordinary ascetic sense—mortifies any disposition to admire
his fellows by dwelling upon the physical necessities which
seem to lower and degrade human pride.   Beauty is but
skin deep ; beneath it is a vile carcase.   He always sees
the " flayed woman " of the *Tale of a Tub*.   The thought
is hideous, hateful, horrible, and therefore it fascinates
him.   He loves to dwell upon the hateful, because it
justifies his hate.   He nurses his misanthropy, as he
might tear his flesh to keep his mortality before his eyes.

The Yahoo is the embodiment of the bestial element
in man ; and Swift in his wrath takes the bestial for
the predominating element.   The hideous, filthy, lustful
monster yet asserts its relationship to him in the most
humiliating fashion : and he traces in its conduct the
resemblance to all the main activities of the human being.
Like the human being it fights and squabbles for the

satisfaction of its lust, or to gain certain shiny yellow stones; it befouls the weak and fawns upon the strong with loathsome compliance; shows a strange love of dirt, and incurs diseases by laziness and gluttony. Gulliver gives an account of his own breed of Yahoos, from which it seems that they differ from the subjects of the Houyhnhnms only by showing the same propensities on a larger scale; and justifies his master's remark that all their institutions are owing to "gross defects in reason and by consequence in virtue." The Houyhnhnms meanwhile represent Swift's Utopia; they prosper and are happy, truthful and virtuous, and therefore able to dispense with lawyers, physicians, ministers and all the other apparatus of an effete civilization. It is in this doctrine, as I may observe in passing, that Swift falls in with Godwin and the revolutionists, though they believed in human perfectibility, whilst they traced every existing evil to the impostures and corruptions essential to all systems of government. Swift's view of human nature, is too black to admit of any hopes of their millennium.

The full wrath of Swift against his species shows itself in this ghastly caricature. It is lamentable and painful, though even here we recognize the morbid perversion of a noble wrath against oppression. One other portrait in Swift's gallery demands a moment's notice. No poetic picture in Dante or Milton can exceed the strange power of his prose description of the Struldbrugs—those hideous immortals who are damned to an everlasting life of drivelling incompetence. It is a translation of the affecting myth of Tithonus into the repulsive details of downright prose. It is idle to seek for any particular moral from these hideous phantoms of Swift's dismal *Inferno*. They embody the terror which

was haunting his imagination as old age was drawing
upon him. The sight, he says himself, should reconcile
a man to death. The mode of reconciliation is terribly
characteristic. Life is but a weary business at best; but,
at least, we cannot wish to drain so repulsive a cup to
the dregs, when even the illusions which cheered us at
moments have been ruthlessly destroyed. Swift was but
too clearly prophesying the melancholy decay into which
he was himself to sink.

The later books of *Gulliver* have been in some sense
excised from the popular editions of the Travels. The
Yahoos, and Houyhnhnms, and Struldbrugs, are indeed
known by name almost as well as the inhabitants of
Lilliput and Brobdingnag; but this part of the book is
certainly not reading for babes. It was probably written
during the years when he was attacking public corruption,
and when his private happiness was being destroyed, when
therefore his wrath against mankind and against his own
fate was stimulated to the highest pitch. Readers who
wish to indulge in a harmless play of fancy will do
well to omit the last two voyages; for the strain of
misanthropy which breathes in them is simply oppressive.
They are probably the sources from which the popular
impression of Swift's character is often derived. It is
important, therefore, to remember that they were wrung
from him in later years, after a life tormented by constant
disappointment and disease. Most people hate the mis-
anthropist even if they are forced to admire his power.
Yet we must not be carried too far by the words. Swift's
misanthropy was not all ignoble. We generally prefer
flattery even to sympathy. We like the man who is blind
to our faults better than the man who sees them and
yet pities our distresses. We have the same kind of

feeling for the race as we have in our own case. We are
attracted by the kindly optimist who assures us that
good predominates in everything and everybody, and
believes that a speedy advent of the millennium must
reward our manifold excellence. We cannot forgive those
who hold men to be "mostly fools," or, as Swift would
assert, mere brutes in disguise, and even carry out that
disagreeable opinion in detail. There is something un-
comfortable and therefore repellent of sympathy in the
mood which dwells upon the darker side of society, even
though with wrathful indignation against the irremovable
evils. Swift's hatred of oppression, burning and genuine
as it was, is no apology with most readers for his perseverance in asserting its existence. "Speak comfortable
things to us" is the cry of men to the prophet in all
ages ; and he who would assault abuses must count upon
offending many who do not approve them, but who would
therefore prefer not to believe in them. Swift, too,
mixed an amount of egoism with his virtuous indignation, which clearly lowers his moral dignity. He really
hates wrongs to his race ; but his sensitiveness is roused
when they are injuries to himself, and committed by his
enemies. The indomitable spirit which made him incapable even of yielding to necessity, which makes him
beat incessantly against the bars which it was hopeless
to break, and therefore waste powers which might
have done good service by aiming at the unattainable,
and nursing grudges against inexorable necessity, limits
our sympathy with his better nature. Yet some of us
may take a different view, and rather pity than condemn
the wounded spirit so tortured and perverted, in consideration of the real philanthropy which underlies the
misanthropy, and the righteous hatred of brutality and

oppression which is but the seamy side of a generous sympathy.   At least we should be rather awed than repelled by this spectacle of a nature of magnificent power struck down, bruised and crushed under fortune, and yet fronting all antagonists with increasing pride, and comforting itself with scorn even when it can no longer injure its adversaries.

CHAPTER IX.

DECLINE.

SWIFT survived his final settlement in Ireland for more than thirty years, though during the last five or six it was but the outside shell of him that lived. During every day in all those years Swift must have eaten and drunk, and somehow or other got through the twenty-four hours. The war against Wood's halfpence employed at most a few months in 1724, and all his other political writings would scarcely fill a volume of this size. A modern journalist who could prove that he had written as little in six months would deserve a testimonial. *Gulliver's Travels* appeared in 1727; and ten years were to pass before his intellect became hopelessly clouded. How was the remainder of his time filled?

The death of Stella marks a critical point. Swift told Gay in 1723 that it had taken three years to reconcile him to the country to which he was condemned for ever. He came back "with an ill head and an aching heart." [1] He was separated from the friends he had loved, and too old to make new friends. A man, as he says elsewhere, [2] who had been bred in a coal-pit might pass his time in it well enough; but if sent back to it after a few months in

[1] To Bolingbroke, May, 1719.
[2] To Pope and Gay, Oct. 15th, 1726.

upper air, he would find content less easy. Swift, in fact,
never became resigned to the " coal-pit," or, to use another
of his phrases, the " wretched, dirty dog-hole and prison,"
of which he could only say that ·it was a "place good
enough to die in."   Yet he became so far acclimatized as
to shape a tolerable existence out of the fragments left to
him.   Intelligent and cultivated men in Dublin, especially
amongst the clergy and the fellows of Trinity College,
gathered round their famous countryman.   Swift formed a
little court ; he rubbed up his classics to the academical
standard, read a good deal of history, and even amused
himself with mathematics.   He received on Sundays at
the deanery, though his entertainments seem to have been
rather too economical for the taste of his guests.   "The
ladies," Stella and Mrs. Dingley, were recognized as more
or less domesticated with him.   Stella helped to receive
his guests, though not ostensibly as mistress of the household ; and, if we may accept Swift's estimate of her social
talents, must have been a very charming hostess.   If some
of Swift's guests were ill at ease in presence of the imperious and moody exile, we may believe that during
Stella's life there was more than a mere semblance of
agreeable society at the deanery.   Her death, as Delany
tells us,[3] led to a painful change.   Swift's temper became
sour and ungovernable ; his avarice grew into a monomania ;
at times he grudged even a single bottle of wine to his
friends ; the giddiness and deafness which had tormented
him by fits, now became a part of his life.   Reading came
to be impossible, because (as Delany thinks) his obstinate
refusal to wear spectacles had injured his sight.   He still
struggled hard against disease ; he rode energetically,

[3] *Delany*, p. 144.

though two servants had to accompany him in case of accidents from giddiness ; he took regular "constitutionals" up and down stairs when he could not go out. His friends thought that he injured himself by over-exercise ; and the battle was necessarily a losing one. Gradually the gloom deepened ; friends dropped off by death, and were alienated by his moody temper ; he was surrounded, as they thought, by designing sycophants. His cousin, Mrs. Whiteway, who took care of him in his last years, seems to have been both kindly and sensible; but he became unconscious of kindness, and in 1741 had to be put under restraint. We may briefly fill up some details in the picture.

Swift at Dublin recalls Napoleon at Elba. The duties of a deanery are not supposed, I believe, to give absorbing employment for all the faculties of the incumbent ; but an empire, however small, may be governed ; and Swift at an early period set about establishing his supremacy within his small domains. He maintained his prerogatives against the archbishop, and subdued his chapter. His inferiors submitted, and could not fail to recognize his zeal for the honour of the body. But his superiors found him less amenable. He encountered episcopal authority with his old haughtiness. He bade an encroaching bishop remember that he was speaking "to a clergyman, and not to a footman." [4] He fell upon an old friend, Sterne, the Bishop of Clogher, for granting a lease to some "old fanatic knight." He takes the opportunity of reviling the bishops for favouring "two abominable bills for beggaring and enslaving the clergy (which took their birth from hell)," and says that he had thereupon resolved to have "no

Bishop of Meath, May 22nd, 1719.

more commerce with persons of such prodigious grandeur, who, I feared, in a little time, would expect me to kiss their slipper." [5] He would not even look into a coach, lest he should see such a thing as a bishop—a sight that would strike him with terror. In a bitter satire he describes Satan as the bishop to whom the rest of the Irish bench are suffragans. His theory was that the English Government always appointed admirable divines, but that unluckily all the new bishops were murdered on Hounslow Heath by highwaymen, who took their robes and patents, and so usurped the Irish sees. It is not surprising that Swift's episcopal acquaintance was limited.

In his deanery Swift discharged his duties with despotic benevolence. He performed the services, carefully criticized young preachers, got his musical friends to help him in regulating his choir, looked carefully after the cathedral repairs, and improved the revenues at the cost of his own interests. His pugnacity broke out repeatedly even in such apparently safe directions. He erected a monument to the Duke of Schomberg after an attempt to make the duke's descendants pay for it themselves. He said that if they tried to avoid the duty by reclaiming the body, he would take up the bones, and put the skeleton " in his register office, to be a memorial of their baseness to all posterity." [6] He finally relieved his feelings by an epitaph, which is a bitter taunt against the duke's relations.

Happily he gave less equivocal proofs of the energy which he could put into his duties. His charity was unsurpassed both for amount and judicious distribution. Delany declares that in spite of his avarice he would give five pounds more easily than richer men would give as many

[5] To Bishop of Clogher, July, 1733.
[6] To Carteret, May 10th, 1728.

shillings. "I never," says this good authority, "saw poor
so carefully and conscientiously attended to in my life as
those of his cathedral." He introduced and carried out
within his own domains a plan for distinguishing the
deserving poor by badges—in anticipation of modern
schemes for "organization of charity." With the first five
hundred pounds which he possessed he formed a fund for
granting loans to industrious tradesmen and citizens, to be
repaid by weekly instalments. It was said that by this
scheme he had been the means of putting more than 200
families in a comfortable way of living.[7] He had, says
Delany, a whole "seraglio" of distressed old women in
Dublin; there was scarcely a lane in the whole city where
he had not such a "mistress." He saluted them kindly,
inquired into their affairs, bought trifles from them, and
gave them such titles as Pullagowna, Stumpa-Nympha, and
so forth. The phrase "seraglio" may remind us of Johnson's establishment, who has shown his prejudice against
Swift in nothing more than in misjudging a charity akin to
his own, though apparently directed with more discretion.
The "rabble," it is clear, might be grateful for other
than political services. To personal dependents he was
equally liberal. He supported his widowed sister, who had
married a scapegrace in opposition to his wishes. He allowed
an annuity of 52*l.* a year to Stella's companion, Mrs.
Dingley, and made her suppose that the money was not a
gift, but the produce of a fund for which he was trustee.
He showed the same liberality to Mrs. Ridgway, daughter
of his old housekeeper, Mrs. Brent; paying her an annuity
of 20*l.*, and giving her a bond to secure the payment in
case of accidents. Considering the narrowness of Swift's

[7] Substance of a speech to the Mayor of Dublin. Franklin left
a sum of money to be employed in a similar way.

income, and that he seems also to have had considerable trouble about obtaining his rents and securing his invested savings, we may say that his so-called "avarice" was not inconsistent with unusual munificence. He pared his personal expenditure to the quick, not that he might be rich, but that he might be liberal.

Though for one reason or other Swift was at open war with a good many of the higher classes, his court was not without distinguished favourites. The most conspicuous amongst them were Delany and Sheridan. Delany (1685—1768), when Swift first knew him, was a Fellow of Trinity College. He was a scholar, and a man of much good feeling and intelligence, and eminently agreeable in society ; his theological treatises seem to have been fanciful, but he could write pleasant verses, and had great reputation as a college tutor. He married two rich wives, and Swift testifies that his good qualities were not the worse for his wealth, nor his purse generally fuller. He was so much given to hospitality as to be always rather in difficulties. He was a man of too much amiability and social suavity not to be a little shocked at some of Swift's savage outbursts, and scandalized by his occasional improprieties. Yet he appreciated the nobler qualities of the staunch, if rather alarming, friend. It is curious to remember that his second wife, who was one of Swift's later correspondents, survived to be the venerated friend of Fanny Burney (1752—1840), and that many living people may thus remember one who was familiar with the latest of Swift's female favourites. Swift's closest friend and crony, however, was the elder Sheridan, the ancestor of a race fertile in genius, though unluckily his son, Swift's biographer, seems to have transmitted without possessing

any share of it. Thomas Sheridan, the elder, was the
typical Irishman—kindly, witty, blundering, full of talents
and imprudences, careless of dignity, and a child in
the ways of the world. He was a prosperous schoolmaster
in Dublin when Swift first made his acquaintance (about
1718), so prosperous as to decline a less precarious post,
of which Swift got him the offer.

After the war of Wood's halfpence Swift became
friendly with Carteret, whom he respected as a man of
genuine ability, and who had besides the virtue of being
thoroughly distrusted by Walpole. When Carteret was
asked how he had succeeded in Ireland, he replied that he
had pleased Dr. Swift. Swift took advantage of the
mutual goodwill to recommend several promising clergy-
men to Carteret's notice. He was specially warm in behalf of Sheridan, who received the first vacant living and
a chaplaincy. Sheridan characteristically spoilt his own
chances by preaching a sermon upon the day of the ac-
cession of the Hanoverian family, from the text, "Sufficient unto the day is the evil thereof." The sermon was
not political, and the selection of the text a pure accident;
but Sheridan was accused of Jacobitism, and lost his
chaplaincy in consequence. Though generously compen-
sated by the friend in whose pulpit he had committed
this "Sheridanism," he got into difficulties. His school
fell off; he exchanged his preferments for others less preferable; he failed in a school at Cavan, and ultimately the
poor man came back to die at Dublin, in 1738, in distressed
circumstances. Swift's relations with him were thoroughly
characteristic. He defended his cause energetically; gave
him most admirably good advice in rather dictatorial
terms; admitted him to the closest familiarity, and
sometimes lost his temper when Sheridan took a liberty

at the wrong moment, or resented the liberties taken by
himself. A queer character of the " Second Solomon,"
written, it seems, in 1729, shows the severity with
which Swift could sometimes judge his shiftless and
impulsive friend, and the irritability with which he
could resent occasional assertions of independence. " He
is extremely proud and captious," says Swift, and " apt to
resent as an affront or indignity what was never intended
for either," but what, we must add, had a strong
likeness to both. One cause of poor Sheridan's troubles
was doubtless that assigned by Swift. Mrs. Sheridan,
says this frank critic, is " the most disagreeable beast in
Europe," a " most filthy slut, lazy, and slothful, luxu-
rious, ill-natured, envious, suspicious," and yet managing
to govern Sheridan. This estimate was apparently
shared by her husband, who makes various references to
her detestation of Swift. In spite of all jars, Swift was
not only intimate with Sheridan and energetic in helping
him, but to all appearance really loved him. Swift came
to Sheridan's house when the workmen were moving the
furniture, preparatory to his departure for Cavan. Swift
burst into tears, and hid himself in a dark closet before he
could regain his self-possession. He paid a visit to his
old friend afterwards ; but was now in that painful and
morbid state in which violent outbreaks of passion made
him frequently intolerable. Poor Sheridan rashly ventured to fulfil an old engagement that he would tell
Swift frankly of a growing infirmity, and said something about avarice. "Doctor," replied Swift, significantly, "did you never read *Gil Blas* ?" When
Sheridan soon afterwards sold his school to return to
Dublin, Swift received his old friend so inhospitably that
Sheridan left him, never again to enter the house. Swift

o

indeed had ceased to be Swift; and Sheridan died soon
afterwards.

Swift often sought relief from the dreariness of the
deanery by retiring to, or rather by taking possession of,
his friends' country-houses.   In 1725 he stayed for some
months, together with "the ladies," at Quilca, a small
country-house of Sheridan's, and compiled an account of
the deficiencies of the establishment—meant to be continued weekly.   Broken tables, doors without locks, a
chimney stuffed with the dean's great-coat, a solitary pair
of tongs forced to attend all the fireplaces and also to
take the meat from the pot, holes in the floors, spikes
protruding from the bedsteads, are some of the items;
whilst the servants are all thieves, and act upon the pro-
verb, "The worse their sty, the longer they lie."   Swift
amused himself here and elsewhere by indulging his taste
in landscape gardening, without the consent and often
to the annoyance of the proprietor.   In 1728—the year
of Stella's death—he passed eight months at Sir Arthur
Acheson's, near Market Hill.   He was sickly, languid, and
anxious to escape from Dublin, where he had no company
but that of his "old presbyterian housekeeper, Mrs.
Brent."   He had, however, energy enough to take the
household in hand after his usual fashion.   He superin-
tended Lady Acheson's studies, made her read to him,
gave her plenty of good advice; bullied the butler;
looked after the dairy and the garden, and annoyed Sir
Arthur by summarily cutting down an old thorn-tree.
He liked the place so much that he thought of building
a house there, which was to be called Drapier's Hall, but
abandoned the project for reasons which, after his fashion,
he expressed with great frankness in a poem.   Probably
the chief reason was the very obvious one which strikes

all people who are tempted to build; but that upon which he chiefly dwells is Sir Arthur's defects as an entertainer. The knight used, it seems, to lose himself in metaphysical moonings when he should have been talking to Swift and attending to his gardens and farms. Swift entered a house less as a guest than a conqueror. His dominion, it is clear, must have become burdensome in his later years, when his temper was becoming savage and his fancies more imperious.

Such a man was the natural prey of sycophants, who would bear his humours for interested motives. Amongst Swift's numerous clients some doubtless belonged to this class. The old need of patronizing and protecting still displays itself; and there is something very touching in the zeal for his friends which survived breaking health and mental decay. His correspondence is full of eager advocacy. Poor Miss Kelly, neglected by an unnatural parent, comes to Swift as her natural adviser. He intercedes on behalf of the prodigal son of a Mr. FitzHerbert in a letter which is a model of judicious and delicate advocacy. His old friend, Barber, had prospered in business; he was Lord Mayor of London in 1733, and looked upon Swift as the founder of his fortunes. To him, "my dear good old friend in the best and worst times," Swift writes a series of letters, full of pathetic utterances of his regrets for old friends amidst increasing infirmities, and full also of appeals on behalf of others. He induced Barber to give a chaplaincy to Pilkington, a young clergyman of whose talent and modesty Swift was thoroughly convinced. Mrs. Pilkington was a small poetess, and the pair had crept into some intimacy at the deanery. Unluckily Swift had reasons to repent his patronage The pair were equally worthless. The husband tried to get a divorce; and the wife sank into misery. One of her last experiments was to publish by subscription certain "Memoirs," which contain some interesting but untrustworthy anecdotes of Swift's later years.[8] He had rather better luck with Mrs. Barber, wife of a Dublin woollendraper, who, as Swift says, was "poetically given, and, for a woman, had a sort of genius that way." He pressed her claims not only upon her namesake, the Mayor, but upon Lord Carteret, Lady Betty Germaine, and Gay and his duchess. A forged letter to Queen Caroline in Swift's name on behalf of this poetess naturally raised some suspicions. Swift, however, must have been convinced of her innocence. He continued his interest in her for years, during which we are glad to find that she gave up poetry for selling Irish linens and letting lodgings at Bath; and one of Swift's last acts before his decay was to present her, at her own request, with the copyright of his *Polite Conversations.* Everybody, she said, would subscribe for a work of Swift's, and it would put her in easy circumstances. Mrs. Barber clearly had no delicacy in turning Swift's liberality to account; but she was a respectable and sensible woman, and managed to bring up two sons to professions. Liberality of this kind came naturally to Swift. He provided for a broken-down old officer, Captain Creichton, by compiling his memoirs for him, to be published by subscription. "I never," he says in 1735, "got a farthing by anything I wrote—except once by Pope's prudent management" This probably refers to *Gulliver*, for which he seems to have received 200*l.* He apparently

---

[8] See also the curious letters from Mrs. Pilkington in Richardson's Correspondence.

gave his share in the profits of the *Miscellanies* to the widow of a Dublin printer.

A few words may now be said about these last writings. In reading some of them, we must remember his later mode of life. He generally dined alone, or with old Mrs. Brent, then sat alone in his closet till he went to bed at eleven. The best company in Dublin, he said, was barely tolerable, and those who had been tolerable were now unsupportable. He could no longer read by candle-light, and his only resource was to write rubbish, most of which he burnt. The merest trifles that he ever wrote, he says in 1731, "are serious philosophical lucubrations in comparison to what I now busy myself about." This, however, was but the development of a lifelong practice. His favourite maxim, *Vive la bagatelle*, is often quoted by Pope and Bolingbroke. As he had punned in his youth with Lord Berkeley, so he amused himself in later years by a constant interchange of trifles with his friends, and above all with Sheridan. Many of these trifles have been preserved ; they range from really good specimens of Swift's rather sardonic humour down to bad riddles and a peculiar kind of playing upon words. A brief specimen of one variety will be amply sufficient. Sheridan writes to Swift. *Times a re veri de ad nota do it oras hi lingat almi e state.* The words separately are Latin, and are to be read into the English : "Times are very dead ; not a doit or a shilling at all my estate." Swift writes to Sheridan in English, which reads into Latin, "Am I say vain a rabble is," means, *Amice venerabilis*—and so forth. Whole manuscript books are still in existence filled with jargon of this kind. Charles Fox declared that Swift must be a goodnatured man to have had such a love of nonsense. We may admit some of it to be a proof

of good-humour in the same sense as a love of the back-
gammon in which he sometimes indulged. It shows, that
is, a willingness to kill time in company. But it must be
admitted that the impression becomes different when we
think of Swift in his solitude wasting the most vigorous
intellect in the country upon ingenuities beneath that of
the composer of double acrostics. Delany declares that
the habit helped to weaken his intellect. Rather it
showed that his intellect was preying upon itself. Once
more we have to think of the "conjured spirit," and the
ropes of sand. Nothing can well be more lamentable.
Books full of this stuff impress us like products of the
painful ingenuity by which some prisoner for life has
tried to relieve himself of the intolerable burden of solitary
confinement. Swift seems to betray the secret when he
tells Bolingbroke that at his age "I often thought of death;
but now it is never out of my mind." He repeats this
more than once. He does not fear death, he says; indeed
he longed for it. His regular farewell to a friend was,
"Good night; I hope I shall never see you again." He
had long been in the habit of "lamenting" his birthday,
though, in earlier days, Stella and other friends had
celebrated the anniversary. Now it became a day of
unmixed gloom, and the chapter in which Job curses the
hour of his birth lay open all day on his table. "And
yet," he says, "I love *la bagatelle* better than ever."
Rather we should say, "and therefore," for in truth the
only excuse for such trifling was the impossibility of
finding any other escape from settled gloom. Friends
indeed seem to have adopted at times the theory that a
humourist must always be on the broad grin. They
called him the "laughter-loving" dean, and thought
Gulliver a "merry book." A strange effect is produced

when between two of the letters in which Swift utters the
bitterest agonies of his soul during Stella's illness, we
have a letter from Bolingbroke to the "three Yahoos of
Twickenham " (Pope, Gay, and Swift), referring to
Swift's " divine science, *la bagatelle*," and ending with
the benediction, "Mirth be with you!" From such
mirth we can only say, may heaven protect us; for it
would remind us of nothing but the mirth of Redgaunt-
let's companions when they sat dead (and damned) at
their ghastly revelry, and their laughter passed into such
wild sounds as made the daring piper's "very nails turn
blue."

It is not, however, to be inferred that all Swift's
recreations were so dreary as this Anglo-Latin, or that his
facetiousness always covered an aching heart. There is
real humour, and not all of bitter flavour, in some of the
trifles which passed between Swift and his friends. The
most famous is the poem called *The Grand Question
Debated*, the question being whether an old building
called Hamilton's Bawn, belonging to Sir A. Acheson, should
be turned into a malthouse or a barrack. Swift takes the
opportunity of caricaturing the special object of his aversion,
the blustering and illiterate soldier, though he indignantly
denies that he had said anything disagreeable to his
hospitable entertainer. Lady Acheson encouraged him
in writing such "lampoons." Her taste cannot have been
very delicate,[9] and she perhaps did not perceive how a
rudeness which affects to be only playful may be really
offensive. If the poem shows that Swift took liberties
with his friends, it also shows that he still possessed the
strange power of reproducing the strain of thought of a
vulgar mind which he exhibited in Mr. Harris's petition.

[9] Or she would hardly have written the *Panegyric.*

Two other works which appeared in these last years are
more remarkable proofs of the same power. *The Complete
Collection of Genteel and Ingenious Conversation* and the
Directions to Servants, are most singular performances,
and curiously illustrative of Swift's habits of thought and
composition. He seems to have begun them during some
of his early visits to England. He kept them by him
and amused himself by working upon them, though they
were never quite finished. The *Polite Conversation* was
given, as we have seen, to Mrs. Barber in his later years,
and the *Directions to Servants* came into the printer's hands
when he was already imbecile. They show how closely
Swift's sarcastic attention was fixed through life upon the
ways of his inferiors. They are a mass of materials for a
natural history of social absurdities such as Mr. Darwin
was in the habit of bestowing upon the manners and
customs of worms. The difference is that Darwin had
none but kindly feelings for worms, whereas Swift's
inspection of social vermin is always edged with contempt. The conversations are a marvellous collection
of the set of cant phrases which at best have supplied
the absence of thought in society. Incidentally there
are some curious illustrations of the customs of the day ;
though one cannot suppose that any human beings had
ever the marvellous flow of pointless proverbs with which
Lord Sparkish, Mr. Neverout, Miss Notable and the rest
manage to keep the ball incessantly rolling. The talk is
nonsensical, as most small-talk would be, if taken down
by a reporter, and, according to modern standard, hide-
ously vulgar, and yet it flows on with such vivacity that it
is perversely amusing.

Lady Answerall. But, Mr. Neverout, I wonder why such a

handsome, straight young gentleman as you don't get some
rich widow?

Lord Sparkish. Straight! Ay, straight as my leg, and
that's crooked at the knee.

Neverout. Truth, madam, if it rained rich widows, none
would fall upon me. Egad, I was born under a threepenny
planet, never to be worth a groat.

And so the talk flows on, and to all appearance might
flow for ever.

Swift professes in his preface to have sat many hundred
times with his table-book ready, without catching a single
phrase for his book in eight hours. Truly he is a kind of
Boswell of inanities; and one is amazed at the quantity of
thought which must have gone into this elaborate trifling
upon trifles. A similar vein of satire upon the emptiness
of writers is given in his *Tritical Essay upon the Faculties
of the Human Mind;* but that is a mere skit compared
with this strange performance. The *Directions to Servants*
shows an equal amount of thought exerted upon the
various misdoings of the class assailed. Some one has
said that it is painful to read so minute and remorseless an
exposure of one variety of human folly Undoubtedly it
suggests that Swift must have appeared to be an omniscient master. Delany, as I have said, testifies to his
excellence in that capacity. Many anecdotes attest
the close attention which he bestowed upon every
detail of his servants' lives, and the humorous reproofs
which he administered. " Sweetheart," he said to an
ugly cookmaid who had overdone a joint, " take this
down to the kitchen and do it less." "That is impossible,"
she replied. " Then," he said, " if you must commit faults,
commit faults that can be mended." Another story tells
how when a servant had excused himself for not cleaning

boots on the ground that they would soon be dirty again,
Swift made him apply the same principle to eating break-
fast, which would be only a temporary remedy for hunger.
In this, as in every relation of life, Swift was under a
kind of necessity of imposing himself upon every one in
contact with him, and followed out his commands into the
minutest details. In the *Directions to Servants* he has
accumulated the results of his experience in one depart-
ment ; and the reading may not be without edification to
the people who every now and then announce as a new
discovery that servants are apt to be selfish, indolent, and
slatternly, and to prefer their own interests to their
master's. Probably no fault could be found with the
modern successors of eighteenth-century servants, which
has not already been exemplified in Swift's presentment
of that golden age of domestic comfort. The details are
not altogether pleasant ; but, admitting such satire to be
legitimate, Swift's performance is a masterpiece.

Swift, however, left work of a more dignified kind. Many
of the letters in his correspondence are admirable specimens
of a perishing art. The most interesting are those which
passed between him, Pope, and Bolingbroke, and which
were published by Pope's contrivance during Swift's last
period. " I look upon us three," says Swift, " as a peculiar
triumvirate, who have nothing to expect or fear, and so
far fittest to converse with one another." We may perhaps
believe Swift when he says that he " never leaned on his
elbow to consider what he should write " (except to fools,
lawyers, and ministers), though we certainly cannot say
the same of his friends. Pope and Bolingbroke are full of
affectations, now transparent enough ; but Swift in a few
trenchant, outspoken phrases, dashes out a portrait of himself as impressive as it is in some ways painful. We must,

indeed, remember in reading his inverse hypocrisy, his
tendency to call his own motives by their ugliest names
—a tendency which is specially pronounced in writing
letters to the old friends whose very names recall the
memories of past happiness, and lead him to dwell upon
the gloomiest side of the present. There is too a characteristic reserve upon some points. In his last visit to
Pope, Swift left his friend's house after hearing the bad
accounts of Stella's health, and hid himself in London
lodgings. He never mentioned his anxieties to his friend,
who heard of them first from Sheridan; and in writing
afterwards from Dublin, Swift excuses himself for the
desertion by referring to his own ill-health—doubtless a
true cause ("two sick friends never did well together ")
—and his anxiety about his affairs, without a word about
Stella. A phrase of Bolingbroke's in the previous year
about "the present Stella, whoever she may be," seems
to prove that he too had no knowledge of Stella except
from the poems addressed to the name. There were
depths of feeling which Swift could not lay bare
to the friend in whose affection he seems most thoroughly to have trusted. Meanwhile he gives full
vent to the scorn of mankind and himself, the bitter
and unavailing hatred of oppression, and above all for
that strange mingling of pride and remorse which is always
characteristic of his turn of mind. When he leaves
Arbuthnot and Pope he expresses the warmth of his feelings by declaring that he will try to forget them. He is
deeply grieved by the death of Congreve, and the grief
makes him almost regret that he ever had a friend. He
would give half his fortune for the temper of an easy-
going acquaintance who could take up or lose a friend as
easily as a cat. "Is not this the true happy man?" The

loss of Gay cuts him to the heart; he notes on the letter
announcing it that he had kept the letter by him five
days "by an impulse foreboding some misfortune." He
cannot speak of it except to say that he regrets that long
living has not hardened him; and that he expects to die
poor and friendless. Pope's ill-health "hangs on his
spirits." His moral is that if he were to begin the world
again, he would never run the risk of a friendship with a
poor or sickly man—for he cannot harden himself.
"Therefore I argue that avarice and hardness of heart
are the two happiest qualities a man can acquire who
is late in his life, because by living long we must lessen
our friends or may increase our fortunes." This bitterness
is equally apparent in regard to the virtues on which he
most prided himself. His patriotism was owing to "perfect rage and resentment, and the mortifying sight of
slavery, folly, and baseness;" in which, as he says, he
is the direct contrary of Pope, who can despise folly and
hate vice without losing his temper or thinking the worse of
individuals. "Oppression tortures him," and means bitter
hatred of the concrete oppressor. He tells Barber in 1738
that for three years he has been but the shadow of his
former self, and has entirely lost his memory, "except
when it is roused by perpetual subjects of vexation." Com-
mentators have been at pains to show that such sentiments
are not philanthropic; yet they are the morbid utterance of
a noble and affectionate nature soured by long misery and
disappointment. They brought their own punishment. The
unhappy man was fretting himself into melancholy and was
losing all sources of consolation. "I have nobody now left
but you," he writes to Pope in 1736; his invention is gone;
he makes projects which end in the manufacture of waste
paper; and what vexes him most is that his "female friends

have now forsaken him." "Years and infirmities," he says
in the end of the same year (about the date of the
Legion Club), "have quite broke me ; I can neither read,
nor write, nor remember, nor converse. All I have left
is to walk and ride." A few letters are preserved in the
next two years—melancholy wails over his loss of health
and spirit—pathetic expressions of continual affection for
his "dearest and almost only constant friend," and a warm
request or two for services to some of his acquaintance.

The last stage was rapidly approaching. Swift who
had always been thinking of death in these later years,
had anticipated the end in the remarkable verses *On the
Death of Dr. Swift*. This and two or three other performances of about the same period, especially the
Rhapsody on Poetry (1733) and the *Verses to a Lady*
are Swift's chief title to be called a poet. How far that
name can be conceded to him is a question of classification. Swift's originality appears in the very fact that
he requires a new class to be made for him. He justified
Dryden's remark in so far as he was never a poet in the
sense in which Milton or Wordsworth or Shelley or
even Dryden himself were poets. His poetry may be
called rhymed prose, and should perhaps be put at about
the same level in the scale of poetry as *Hudibras*. It
differs from prose not simply in being rhymed, but in
that the metrical form seems to be the natural and
appropriate mode of utterance. Some of the purely
sarcastic and humorous phrases recall *Hudibras* more
nearly than anything else ; as, for example, the often-
quoted verses upon small critics in the *Rhapsody.*

> The vermin only tease and pinch
> Their foes superior by an inch.

> So, naturalists observe a flea
> Has smaller fleas that on him prey,
> And these have smaller still to bite 'em,
> And so proceed *ad infinitum.*

In the verses on his own death, the suppressed passion, the glow and force of feeling which we perceive behind the merely moral and prosaic phrases seem to elevate the work to a higher level. It is a mere running of every-day language into easy-going verse; and yet the strangely mingled pathos and bitterness, the peculiar irony of which he was the great master, affect us with a sentiment which may be called poetical in substance, more forcibly than far more dignified and in some sense imaginative performances. Whatever name we may please to give to such work, Swift has certainly struck home and makes an impression which it is difficult to compress into a few phrases. It is the essence of all that is given at greater length in the correspondence; and starts from a comment upon Rochefoucauld's congenial maxim about the misfortunes of our friends. He tells how his acquaintance watch his decay, tacitly congratulating themselves that "it is not yet so bad with us;" how, when he dies, they laugh at the absurdity of his will.

> To public uses! there's a whim!
> What had the public done for him?
> Mere envy, avarice, and pride,
> He gave it all—but first he died.

Then we have the comments of Queen Caroline and Sir Robert and the rejoicings of Grub Street at the chance of passing off rubbish by calling it his. His friends are really touched.

> Poor Pope will grieve a month, and Gay
> A week, and Arbuthnot a day,
> St. John himself will scarce forbear
> To bite his pen and drop a tear,
> The rest will give a shrug and cry,
> " 'Tis pity, but we all must die!"

The ladies talk over it at their cards. They have learnt to show their tenderness, and

> Receive the news in doleful dumps.
> The dean is dead (pray what is trumps?);
> Then, Lord have mercy on his soul!
> (Ladies, I'll venture for the *vole*).

The poem concludes, as usual, with an impartial character of the dean. He claims, with a pride not unjustifiable, the power of independence, love of his friends, hatred of corruption and so forth; admits that he may have had "too much satire in his vein," though adding the very questionable assertion that he "lashed the vice but spared the name." Marlborough, Wharton, Burnet, Steele, Walpole and a good many more might have had something to say upon that head. The last phrase is significant,—

> He gave the little wealth he had
> To build a house for fools and mad;
> And showed by one satiric touch
> No nation needed it so much,
> That kingdom he hath left his debtor,
> I wish it soon may have a better!

For some years, in fact, Swift had spent much thought and time in arranging the details of this bequest. He ultimately left about 12,000*l*., with which, and some other

contributions, St. Patrick's Hospital was opened for fifty
patients in the year 1757.

The last few years of Swift's life were passed in an
almost total eclipse of intellect. One pathetic letter to
Mrs. Whiteway gives almost the last touch. "I have been
very miserable all night, and to-day extremely deaf and
full of pain. I am so stupid and confounded that I cannot express the mortification I am under both of body and
mind. All I can say is that I am not in torture ; but I
daily and hourly expect it. Pray let me know how your
health is and your family. I hardly understand one word
I write. I am sure my days will be very few, for miserable they must be. If I do not blunder, it is Saturday,
July 26, 1740. If I live till Monday, I shall hope to see
you, perhaps for the last time." Even after this he
occasionally showed gleams of his former intelligence, and
is said to have written a well-known epigram during an
outing with his attendants :—

> Behold a proof of Irish sense !
> Here Irish wit is seen !
> When nothing's left that's worth defence
> They build a magazine.

Occasionally he gave way to furious outbursts of violent
temper ; and once suffered great torture from a swelling in
the eye. But his general state seems to have been
apathetic ; sometimes he tried to speak, but was unable to
find words. A few sentences have been recorded. On
hearing that preparations were being made for celebrating
his birthday, he said, "It is all folly ; they had better
let it alone." Another time he was heard to mutter, "I am
what I am ; I am what I am." Few details have been
given of this sad period of mental eclipse ; nor can we

regret their absence. It is enough to say that he suffered occasional tortures from the development of the brain-disease; though as a rule he enjoyed the painlessness of torpor. The unhappy man lingered till the 19th of October, 1745, when he died quietly at three in the afternoon, after a night of convulsions. He was buried in St. Patrick's Cathedral, and over his grave was placed an epitaph, containing the last of those terrible phrases which cling to our memory whenever his name is mentioned. Swift lies, in his own words,—

> Ubi sæva indignatio
> Cor ulterius lacerare nequit.

What more can be added?

THE END.

P

LONDON :
GILBERT AND RIVINGTON, LIMITED,
ST. JOHN'S SQUARE.

For EU product safety concerns, contact us at Calle de José Abascal, 56–1°, 28003 Madrid, Spain or eugpsr@cambridge.org.